To Catch a Trout

To Catch a Trout

NORMAN STRUNG

Drawings by C. W. "Wally" Hansen

Photos by Norman and Sil Strung

STEIN AND DAY/*Publishers*/New York

Library of Congress Cataloging in Publication Data

Strung, Norman.
    To catch a trout.

    Includes index.
    1.   Trout fishing.   I.   Title.
SH687.S82   799.1'7'55   78-24561
ISBN 0-8128-2574-8

DEDICATION

Frank Abbey, Tony Accerano, Wayland Adams, Stu Apte, Joe Arata, Jack Barsness, John Barsness, Dave Beasley, Jean Bergman, Willie The Bohunk, Bud Brackett, Ed Burlingame, Bill Burmeister, Billy Byrnes, Willie Claussen, Holly Croy, Sam Curtis, Jay Feldman, Francis Fortier, Doug Gillespie, George Goldstein, George Haffa, Bob Hodges, Walt Hodges, Bill Hoerschgen, Sandy Jennewein, Paul Jesswein, Frank Johnson, Carrol Kaup, Ralph Kaup, Oscar Kovalovsky, Mary Langan, Iron Mike Levine, Chris LoCascio, Bill Long, Jim Long, Waldo Maffei, Ben Masters, Nels McKenzie, Roy Morsch, Jim Myers, Ed St. Cin, Fred Scholl, Ed Seitz, Tom Sicard, John Silver, Nan Silver, Hal Smith, Joe Smith, Oscar Spangarood, Eli Spannagel, Don Stevens, August C. Strung, August M. Strung, Carlos Torres, Tony Torres, Dick Van Riper, Toad Watson, David Weden, Dick Weden, Joe Wigley, Lee Wulff, Dave Wolny, Joe Yankoskie, Bob Yaskulski. . . . I've learned about trout fishing from all of you.

Other Books by the Author

The Hunter's Almanac
The Fisherman's Almanac (with Dan Morris)
Family Fun Around the Water (with Dan Morris)
Camping in Comfort (with Sil Strung)
Spin-Fishing (with Milt Rosko)
Deer Hunting
Whitewater! (with Sam Curtis and Earl Perry)
Misty Mornings and Moonless Nights
Communicating the Outdoor Experience (editor)
An Encyclopedia of Knives
The Complete Hunter's Catalog

*Give me a fish and I will have a meal
Teach me to fish and I will eat forever*

—Japanese proverb

*Be not too tame neither
    but let your own discretion be your tutor
suit the action to the word
    the word to the action
with this special observance
    that you o'erstep not
the modesty of nature*

—Shakespeare, "Hamlet"

Contents

Introduction

The nestlings born of the hen robin who took up residency outside my window last month are yawning toward a fat worm, Quicksilver Creek is roaring with run-off, and the grass is greener than Ireland. It is a good time to develop a frame of mind about a trout book.

But every time I try to set things straight, something keeps intruding. Logic dictates a dry methodology; a chapter-by-chapter examination of trout tackle, fishing techniques, and the habits and habitat of each species of Salmo and Salvelinus, yet when I arrange racks of rods in my mind they seem wooden, instead of alive and responsive as they do in my hand. I lose an essential dimension of a brook trout by reducing it to a Latin name and a pattern of behavior. When I seek to set down the steps by which one learns how to flycast, something inside me whispers "no, that is not the way."

The unease that is riding on my back is a sense of the unnatural; that I am missing something important about troutfishing in the distance set by the first and third person, the traditional medium of expository writing. I am missing the second person: you.

This is surely a matter of habit, and I know how it was formed. A book about how to catch a trout is really a kind of textbook, a lesson, a mode of teaching, and I have been a teacher most of my working life, as a university instructor, and as a fishing guide. First as a pupil, then as a teacher, there has always been the human element associated with my troutfishing, and ultimately, a new friendship. If I am to be comfortable, and accurate, and true in this book, then you must be included in the book, too.

So I have decided to take you troutfishing, to spend a day with you no differently than if you had hired my services as a guide. To speak with you rather than at you, so that we can get to know each other as well as the trout we seek. In some ways, the two kinds of knowledge are inseparable; in many ways, you will find them enriching.

We will fish a mythical wonder of a stream that flows from the imagination, but that encompasses all the conditions of troutfishing that I have witnessed in these United States. A fiction? Perhaps by definition, but a necessary form that in no way suggests an untruth. The freedom of fiction provides the opportunity for an accuracy that surpasses fact.

So pack a lunch and I will meet you in a few moments. In the meanwhile you should know a little more of how I feel about troutfishing. We will be together all day, and speaking from personal experience, I have found that not everyone agrees with the way I choose to catch a trout.

To Catch a Trout

Prologue

To catch a trout is a celebration of joy, like fireworks, Christmas, and making love; a celebration that transcends time, mind, and place to unite all three in a dazzling moment of silver compression.

I cannot say precisely when the moment begins, but it starts to tick soon after you perceive the current boil, the dimpling rise, the sullen shadow that suggests a finning fish. At that point, the world shrinks to a small circle of stream and self with a trout at the center. Vision tunnels around your cast, then time stretches and flows like a honey river as you throw to the spot and the sharp gift drifts down.

Images and seconds collide with the strike. If it is to be believed that life passes in front of you at the moment of death, then this part is a little like dying. Polygraphs and seismographs go off the paper, yet the bristling points of every detail are as clear and as hard as diamond; the hammer blow, the genuflecting rod, the fractured blasts of a thousand bits of sunlight. Time remains frozen there until you know that you are connected, then it begins to melt as anticipation starts its slow ebb toward reality.

The trout pumps and works, tugging at the line, and your union is affirmed by a 200-mile network of nerves. There remain elements of wonder, fear and doubt: how big is the fish, will it break off, will the hook pull out before he is yours? But the main charge has been sparked. One by one, subjective pleasures fall to deliberate mechanics; a conscious evaluation of when to apply pressure, when to take in line, and objective speculations on the dimensions and breeding of the fish.

The wild graph of time begins to approach normal. It curves and sweeps once again as the trout nears the rim of the net and flicks his tail, but by the time he is safe within its geometric folds, sixty seconds fit perfectly within the bracket of a minute. Vision has regained periphery, and the circle breaks like a soap bubble, but only temporarily. It will form again after the next cast, in the next hour, or under the boughs of the hemlock ahead.

Like a rise on calm water, this trout forms the nucleus, the center, but the ripples ring out to add texture, drama, and color, successive circles of value that are an intrinsic part of the whole; the ambience of the stream-world, and the excellence of a perfect rod. The physical and intellectual satisfaction of a well-wrought cast, the recollection of other fish and other places, the promise of a warm fire in an old cabin when the night has come, fishing partners, current and lost.

The temptation is to cite statistics and records and line weights, but vignettes intrude. Like the day on the Gunflint River when caddis flies swirled like snow through a sunset so rich you could hold it in your hand. The fish went insane, and just as the light faded to a point where I couldn't distinguish my fly, a ponderous brown sucked it in. We stayed inside our world for fifteen minutes, and I finally lost him to a hitch around the accursed duckweed that grows like giant horsetails from the

bottom of that river. I remember a profound sense of exhaustion, but not of loss.

There have been victories too, and one of the sweetest I can remember was one of my first. It was recorded in a tidal pool not more than an acre in size, within an hour's drive of New York City. The fishing pressure was tremendous there, but so was my teen-age determination. I cast, and studied, and learned by the light of a hundred gray dawns, and on an April morning I hooked and landed a 3-pound salter on 2-pound ultralight gear and a CP Swing spinner. "Worms," the pool veterans had insisted, "is all they'll bite on." But I had seen a killie being chased through the brackish water, and the moment started ticking away.

Then there was the day when young Carlos and I caught a fat 6-inch brookie from Quicksilver Creek. We parted some grass and found a worm, and I rigged it below a tiny splitshot on a length of monofilament. We crawled to the creek bank, and, while we lay on our bellies, I dropped the bait into a bank eddy.

"There he is, Carlos," I whispered in Spanish as the rapping began. He touched the line and then took hold as I withdrew my hand. His eyes narrowed and a mysterious smile tugged at the corners of his mouth. He had moved inside a circle too.

Are some moments better than others? I am tempted to say yes; that the finest, most memorable encompass an acrobatic rainbow, a slick-topped river on a June afternoon, and a dry-fly; but I would not deny the same fish, hooked on a nymph in a lake, the purity of his battle, devoid of the interference of current, and the reflection of his image as he vaults above a mirror of calm water.

Nor could I ignore the pleasure of his company on a spinning lure that he has struck with such ferocity that I fear for the flimsy line. Or will I ever cease to marvel at the possibilities of his identity, while he gnaws away at a fat worm on the bottom of a spring-swollen stream.

The implications are clear. The trout in the middle is the

essence of my pleasures, and catching him by hook and line their consummation. Ripples ring out, some perhaps more distinct than others, but they are effect, not cause. They lead the eye and the mind to the target, but the moment is lost without a center.

To fish is to catch a fish. To fish for a trout is to catch a trout, and to that end, I will tumble from the lofty heights of dry-fly purism like Dante through hell. If they refuse my floating fly, I try a nymph, if they refuse a nymph, a lure, and if they refuse a lure you will eventually find me groveling on my knees along the stream bank, searching for some hopping, slithering, crawling sign of what it is they want that day. Whatever sign may be given, I accept it humbly, and use it. The joy is to catch a trout.

It is not a self-contradiction, however, to say that I can enjoy troutfishing, and catch nothing. The element here is that the chance for victory, the chance for the moment, must be there. So long as I have tapped my every resource to imitate and complement the natural scheme of woods, water, and air as I perceive it, I can lose myself for a while. I am good for an average of 15 minutes per pool, at a terminal tackle exchange rate of once every 5 minutes. Depending on the strength of the sun and the depth of the sky, the quality of birdsong and the water ahead, I will stay with the game for between 45 minutes and three hours. If I find neither fish nor encouragement, I conclude they're not biting, and quit.

A bad day? Never. Moments have been launched, my vision has tunneled, and I have been absorbed in periods of intense concentration to the exclusion of all but my immediate surroundings. It has been relaxing.

But it has not been satisfying. For that to happen, I must catch a fish, and that abiding principle is where we will begin, you and I. Nothing special, nothing unusual, just one way in a million to catch a trout; a story of decline, fall, and the infinite pleasures you're likely to find inside a circle. Just a way that happens to be mine.

1 / Finding It

Have we met before? I think so. I play hell to remember names, but I don't have a bad memory for faces, and yours is familiar. Did I bump into you duck-hunting last season? Or maybe it was deer-hunting? No, now I remember. It was late one evening last spring, and the woods were dark. We both had stayed a little longer than might have been wise . . . there was a marvelous hatch of duns coming off . . . and you weren't sure if you were on the right path. Then my black lab showed up out of nowhere and startled you. That was the connection with hunting; the woods and the dog.

It looks like you are going fishing again. You should do quite well. This time of year, this week in fact, is when troutfishing should be at its best. There's a connection with natural order. Everything is growing at its most rapid rate; the grass, the leaves, the flowers, the young of wildlife. And trout react to it too. I caught six in a little over an hour last night, one of them a 16-

inch rainbow. Superb fishing, and in a place that's rumored to be fished out.

... I'm sorry you asked that question. I cannot tell you, or more accurately, I will not. It's nothing personal, understand, just that I think a trout deserves more than to be given away, advertised like so much hamburger at a supermarket sale. I have my reasons, too.

It is to my discredit that I have given away too many fish. I'm not talking about the pan-sized brookies I bring to Jim Long, or the home-smoked rainbows I give friends at Christmas, I mean thousands, perhaps tens of thousands of trout that I gave away for no reason at all, and to people I didn't even know.

Worse, my frivolous actions have had greater consequences than just trout wasted. There are muddy paths trampled in the dewy grasses along Limestone Spring Creek. You can't find a parking spot along the Fishskill on a weekend. The limit on the Roaring River dropped from 10 to three trout this year.

I've been told this is an irreversible trend of the future. People have more money and more leisure time, so there will be more fishermen. To accomodate them, we must sacrifice solitude, style, and freedom. I cannot debate that there are more trout fishermen now than 10 years ago, or fault the logic that suggests there will be more 10 years from now. But I do not agree that the numbers of fishermen alone are at the core of the problem and its questionable solution.

The more I wrestle with the status of troutfishing today, the more I become convinced that the real threat to its survival, as we know and idealize it, is mass communication. Not through the exchange of ideas and knowledge, or the recounting of victories and defeats, but in the naming of names and marking of places. It is an attack on troutfishing from the rear.

"The Marble River, from milepost 13 to 16, is a sure bet for big browns on a #14 Blue Dun in the evenings."

How often have you read that line? How often have I repeated it? And what have either of us gained?

Perhaps you went up to the Marble River, and caught a few of those big browns. Did they really amount to much more than casting practice? In fact, those parched lines you read probably stole three-fourths of the enchantment of catching those fish; the absorbing speculation, the exercise of intellect, the rich satisfaction that comes from a success based on understanding and independent thought.

And how about the brown? Have I ennobled him or his environment by making him easy prey? In the twilight of your confrontation, were you aware of the feel of the water around you and the timelessness of a river? Connected to him by a slender thread, could you feel the perfection of his battle, and were you awed by his genetic excellence? Probably not. It's unusual to notice things like that when you are given a fish.

And what have I done to the Marble? Put another nail in her coffin of public admiration. A river can be loved to death. By the mere act of repetition, reputation builds to reknown. The Roaring River, the Fishskill, the Marble, thus become catchwords that are synonymous with troutfishing. The faithful flock to their shores and trample the grass. Pressure forces changes if there is to be any fishing at all; catch-and-release, flyfishing only, reservations please. Benign tyrannies, but not troutfishing anymore.

I must equate troutfishing with freedom, and call freedom one of its essential qualities, so I will no longer give away fish or rivers, and imprison the sport. Selfish? In a way, perhaps, but selfish for us all. There is still real troutfishing, near-wilderness trout fishing, 65 miles from New York City. I have found a place where I could be alone, and meet a trout on his own terms within an hour's drive of all the big-name waters I have fished. A few of them have been suggested to me by close friends. Most I have found on my own. Discoveries like these are as sweet as the fishing I have enjoyed there, for they are personal, and as much a part of the fishing as the trout I seek.

So don't ask me to tell you names and places. I will not give away trout. I am sorry.

I see you are smiling and nodding. I'm glad you understand. It's much better when you "fish on your own hook." That's an odd expression, I know, but it is a favorite of mine. I learned it from old Oscar Spangarood. He's gone now, but he taught me a great deal about fishing in his broken English. I once asked him if he had ever been a commercial fisherman in Norway . . . he seemed to know how fish thought . . . and he said, "No, I always fish on my own hook." It's a good attitude to take.

I'm beginning to remember more about that night now . . . we sat there by the car and talked about troutfishing and dogs, and my lab kept nudging your hand. He really liked you, and he's an excellent judge of character. When you left, I realized that I'd never asked your name; I was sorry because I would have liked to have fished with you someday.

Tell you what. I was going fishing myself. A party had to cancel out at the last moment, and I just couldn't resist the promise of this day. If I wouldn't be imposing, I'll join up with you, and maybe I can give you a few pointers. Just the other day, Lyle Ferguson said something that stuck; that there don't seem to be any more uncles, or fathers, or grandfathers who hunt and fish. "Who is going to teach, not just fishing, but love, and respect for wild things, and sportsmanship?" So I won't give you a fish, but maybe I can teach you how to catch one. I won't tell you about places, just principles. Then you can make the discoveries on your own. It is a much greater gift.

Besides, you can't really trust most word-of-mouth tips from strangers about where to go. You usually get sent off to some place that is terrible fishing. I've got to admit that the idea crossed my mind when you first asked, but I thought better of it. It's not really fair.

Tackleshops? Common sense might suggest that they are a good place to start looking for trout, but I once worked in one. Since then, I have investigated them casually from the other side of the counter. I have never heard or been given information in a tackleshop that transcended misleading half-truths. Something like, "The fish are taking Kamlooper spoons in the Marble River."

That kind of recommendation stems from the fact that three days ago, a guy came in with his limit from the Marble, and he said he caught them on gold spoons. Kamloopers are suggested specifically, because they are the most expensive lures in the store. Still, there is more to the story.

What really happened was that the fellow knocked 'em dead on Back Brook with a #12 Royal Coachman, but he wouldn't give that information to his grandmother, so he said he caught them on the Marble because he never fishes there anyway.

And you really can't blame him. Would you make information like that available to a hundred total strangers? Of course not! It is like selling your birthright for a bowl of porridge. And even if the proprietor were given accurate information, the chances are one in ten that he'd pass it on to you, because as soon as five o'clock rolls around, he's going to close up shop and race over to Back Brook, hoping that the guy who told him about it in the first place has developed bursitis in his casting arm by now.

Word-of-mouth information from strangers is more than unreliable, it is a strong suggestion that you will find the best fishing by going the other way. If someone ever does put you on to a stream that is paved with the backs of finning trout, count him as a friend, cherish him forever, and don't tell another soul.

You're wiser to do just what you're doing: go for a ride in the country. An old, winding road that weaves a path through farms and forests and the freshness of a spring morning. By the way, did you see the grouse and her clutch by the roadside a moment ago? Remember this place next fall. And look there, at the edge of the field . . . a cock pheasant picking grit. They're pretty in the fall, but in the spring the brilliance and depth of their colors makes you catch your breath. Come to think of it, I've never hunted up here off the riverbottom, and I don't know why. It looks perfect, with the hedgerows between the fields, and all that corn. Quite a view too. That hazy mountain way off in the distance is in the next state! It looks like we both might make some important discoveries before this day is over.

Do you know that you can tell a lot about a trout stream just by looking at it? A little like the way those two birds said something about hunting this fall. It's a profitable craft to master. If you think every trout stream and lake worth fishing has a public identity, you are very wrong. The Gunflint River just might be the best trout stream in the nation. It has a greater concentration of trout up to seven pounds, per acre-foot of water, than any stream on record. A public highway crosses it, and though much of it is posted, I have never been refused permission to fish there when I asked. I've never seen the Gunflint mentioned by name ... it's real name ... in angling literature.

The Goldfish Bowl is a little pond with marly shallows; it is less than 100 yards across and a mile long. It curls along the floor of a narrow valley three miles away from one of the nation's most heavily fished streams. In that stream it is a good day when you catch half a dozen 12-inch trout. I have stood on the huge, buff boulder that rests in the middle of the Goldfish Bowl and had that many fish follow my lure at once; great bullets of brown trout, with gold sides and brilliant orange spotting that glowed like the sun.

Both places were personal discoveries that evolved from a sense of curiosity, and a cognizance of the outward signs that point to a trout stream's inward grace. Let me tell you some of the measurements I use.

Streams that ripple through a vision of green are as suggestive as erotic art. Trust your instincts. If streams look inviting, with slow, slick currents that meander like a snake, and tall, comfortable trees that bow to brush the water, trout will find them attractive too. Ask the question: would you like to live there?

Lush bank vegetation, thick grass, thatches of brush, and trees that tower at the water's edge also translate into root networks that help to stabilize the stream during periods of high water. In more gentle times, those roots serve to reinforce undercuts and they create tangles where trout can rest and hide.

Low, sweeping branches make for shade during the dog days of summer, when the August sun might otherwise raise water temperatures above a trout's tolerance level. Their deep, inner shadows serve as camouflage and safe feeding stations for trout too, and frustration for fishermen. You get convinced that they, more than any other place in the stream, harbor the most, biggest, and hungriest trout, because you can never get to them.

That's another thing. A very good trout stream will always have some water that is impossible to fish; tangles of snags and sweepers on sharp bends, or thick thatches of willow laced along the shore. Cover like that acts as a kind of trout bank. When you take a fish from an accessible station in a stream, another one will move into it from "the bank." Don't kid yourself. Trout are tuned into their environment, and territorial. They know how to find a place to fin that will bring them the most food with the least effort, and they'll defend that spot against any intruder. That's why being able to read water is so important. When you can identify the richest station in a section of stream, you also have found the largest trout; then, when you catch him, another will take his place. That's like the Breakfast Pool on Quicksilver Creek. It's a small place, no bigger than a bedroom, but every time I fish it, I know it is good for at least one brookie. It's an open, slow-moving eddy right between two sections of stream that are almost impassable, because of the thickness of the bankbrush.

But brush does even more. An abundance of any kind of plant life along the shore also means an abundance of land insects, a secondary food source to complement aquatic varieties. Banks that are lined with trees and grass regularly funnel crickets, grasshoppers, worms, beetles, grubs, hellgrammites, spiders and other nightmares into the water. Terrestrials seldom account for the major portion of a trout's diet, but they do represent additional energy that eventually translates into a stream's carrying capacity.

Now there's something else I've learned. Not to come this far when there's snow on the ground. This is some steep grade into the valley . . . an ear popper . . . and it's a northern exposure too. The sun probably never hits the pavement between October and April.

The place is interesting though. There . . . the end of the pavement. Lighter traffic beyond here, and there is sure to be a stream at the bottom of a valley this big. As a matter of fact, I see an old wooden bridge up ahead. Pull onto it, and let's see what the water looks like.

Listen to it groan and creak, and the slats bang around under your tires. Kind of a comfortable sound, like rolling over in an old, brass bed. You've got radials I'll bet. Great tires, but noisy as a tin roof in a hailstorm.

What do you think? I like the look of it, the feel of it. Dark and green and framed by trees, almost a little mysterious. And look. . . . there against the bank, where dark shadows are in contrast to the morning sunlight. See the flies buzzing around? That's a good indication of stream fertility too. The richer the water, the more insects it will hold. They're the real barometer of stream quality, kind of the bottom line as far as trout are concerned, because their nymphal stages are in the water all year long. If a stream is polluted, or short on oxygen, or gets too warm in the summer, insects can't live, and trout can't either. But when you see a lot of aquatics, it suggests good water and plenty of food.

Let me tell you one of my secrets. I'm a stream watcher. When fishing is slow, or I want to take a break, I just sit along the bank and watch. I don't really look at one thing, I try to look at everything; the whole picture. The way the water moves, its texture, the patterns of reflections, the banks' shadows, the air, the shapes of rocks and trees . . . it's not just opening your eyes,

it's opening your head. You'd be amazed at what you can see when you really look. Take those flies.

I can remember one day on the Gunflint. It was late afternoon, and the sunrays were slanting into the stream corridor. The shadows were long and leaden but in the sun the highlights were dazzling. If you looked toward the shadows, you could see swarms of flies. They stood out like fireflies at dusk. Tiny midges that numbered in the thousands skated across the surface of the stream, turning and circling in an ice ballet. Above them, like a windpuff ravaging a field of ripe dandelions, caddis, mayflies, and dragonflies whirled and stopped and smacked the water. Two stoneflies that were mating fell into the stream at my feet, an inchworm dropped off a tree and into my lap, a tent caterpillar drifted by, and I was constantly sparring with mosquitos.

The effect was surreal. The air, the trees, the water, pulsed with a fury of life, and although I knew the Gunflint to be a remarkable trout stream, if I had never heard its name before, its excellence was suggested by that moment.

So let's stream-watch for a few moments. Just sit on the bridge and let the river ramble on. Here is something interesting already. A dragonfly emerging from its nymphal case. Did you ever witness that little bit of magic? The size of the fly and the tiny prison from which it came? And those cabbage wings. They will stretch and smooth and grow to full length in an hour. This place we've found is looking better by the moment, but there are still other things to consider.

Plant life and insect life aren't the only units of measurement that define a trout stream. See how this one winds? Watercourses that twist, turn, and meander make for better habitat than those that run straight. There is the matter of compression . . . more water in a mile of wrinkled stream than in a mile of straight stream . . . and the resulting increase in land-based food that is the consequence of more bank area. Just as important though, is the variety of hiding places that are created when a river wanders: cut banks, rotating eddies, point bars, and riffles. Meander-

Dragonfly emerging from its nymphal case

ing water is also slow water, and slow water means more fish.

The archetypal trout stream is a racing ribbon of crystal, fast, clean, and cold. In fact, streams of this character make a debatable trout habitat. Fast water carves a relatively straight, even bed, without comfortable eddies or slow, deep pools. It also conflicts with the establishment of bank vegetation. Busy streams usually fill to their banks only during high-water periods. At other times, they have a margin of pebbles and cobbles that stretch from the water's edge to the plant community along the bank. This limits the contribution land-based foods can make to the patterns of aquatic life.

Energy conversion rates also enter the picture. It takes a lot more food to raise and maintain a 12-inch trout living in a 6-knot current than one in a 2-knot current. Trout have to work harder to cope with swift water. It's like living on a treadmill.

Quicksilver Creek is that kind of treadmill. It heads up in the high country at a series of spring-fed rills that fall to the valley below like bridal veils. Once it gathers itself up, it tumbles down Quicksilver Canyon, past douglas fir and lodgepole pine, then through cottonwood and quaking asp as elevation enforces the natural transition from forest to plains. It is a beautiful, changing little stream; one that roars in the spring, and then makes noises like a muted xylophone during summer days. I fish it often, and little Quicksilver has become my leisure, my laboratory, and, in a way, mine alone. I can count the fishermen I've seen there on the finger of one hand.

There is a reason. The trout Quicksilver raises are small. The largest fish she ever gave up was a 14-inch rainbow, and 10-inch brookies are more the average. But I believe in the small-can-be-beautiful school of philosophy, and fishing Quicksilver with the lightest of tackle is the most genuine pleasure I can imagine.

When we first discovered each other, however, her fish weren't even that big. There were a glut of 4- to 6-inch brookies, and a rare 10-inch rainbow, usually stationed under an unapproachable tangle of branches and brush. More from the frustration of trying to penetrate barriers with a cast than the notion that slowing down the water would improve the fishing, I started to build dams. They were neither large nor permanent, just a bunch of boulders rolled across the stream that raised the water behind them a foot or two. And I had to rebuild them each spring, after high water. But they slowed the creek down, and created an atmosphere where fish didn't have to fight the current quite so much. I started catching more and bigger fish. It was a dramatic change, too. Numbers and size showed a definable increase in five months.

Now the place amounts to a private paradise. After five years of building those dams, it's not unusual for me to take a dozen perfect trout in a quarter-mile of stream.

No, we don't know what kind of water lies above here, but from the look of the bed, and the pool downstream, it appears to be an excellent environment for trout. Let me show you something else. How wide would you say this stream is? Thirty feet? I would agree. Now, how far would you judge the distance to be between the first meander upstream and the next one below the bridge? About 60 to 70 yards, right?

It is a rule of thumb that moving water ideally suited to trout produces, as a natural consequence, a meander in its bed at a ratio of one-to-seven. When meanders are spaced apart at roughly seven times the width of a stream, this suggests a perfect harmony between brook and trout.

But water temperatures have an even stronger influence. How and why is easy to explain, but hard to evaluate just by standing here. The coolness that you feel around you is enough to let you know that this place is right for trout now, but it doesn't tell us anything about July and August maximums. They're the real factor in trout survival, just as winter forage is for wildlife.

I've found that the outer temperature limits of trout fishing lie around 35 and 75 degrees. Trout can survive in water below 35, but they are torpid. I've coaxed them to bite on bait, but it's always been slow fishing, and inhospitable as an ice bath in an igloo. And when you pull them from water this cold, they are about as lively as a stone you snagged from the bottom.

Above 75 degrees, trout go into seclusion. Any higher temperatures than these are flirting with their tolerance level, and they seek out the minute differences in temperature occasioned by deep shadows, large boulders, and the bottom. Survival is the foremost of their instincts at this time, so they show diminished interest in food. Seventy-five degree water is also a signal for more profound concern than whether or not the fish are biting. Unless its occurrence in a particular stream is truly rare, it's a sign of deteriorating habitat. Usually denuded banks, siltation, and improper industrial use of water, or some combination of the three, are at the bottom of the problem. Thermal pollution is what it's called, and unless it is corrected, trout will eventually be cooked right out of the stream. I've seen it happen too. There's a river west of here that I once would have called the best of them all. I used to float it a lot, and it wasn't unusual for one boat to take thirty trout in a morning, some of them four and five pounds. But an old reservoir, midway along its course, finally silted in to a point where the sun, on really hot summer days, raises the temperature on the flats so that the water at the outflow hits 80 degrees.

I've watched that river die. In 10 years, clear water turned pastel green with an algae bloom, and a thick carpet of moss sprouted from every rock in the river. The moss now tears loose in spidery balls to foul lines and the guts of the trout. The kype-jawed browns that whaled at my hook in every pool are but a handful now. I don't go there anymore. It is like watching an old friend succumb to cancer.

But this place looks more encouraging. Water that hangs between 55 and 70 degrees rates as a perfect environment. Trout feed most actively and grow the fastest surrounded by those kinds of temperatures, and my guess would be that this stream has them. The big shade trees are the clue; they mellow the heat of the sun. Of course, it surely drops well below those temperatures in the winter, but that doesn't hurt the fish. They just grow more slowly. Temperatures, incidentally, are one reason why spring creeks make for such great fishing. They boil up from the ground at around 52 degrees, even in the winter, so that trout are growing and active all the time.

You know, I get the feeling that maybe I'm sounding too absolute, too rigid. I'm actually talking about ideals. If a river doesn't have a lot of bankbrush, or if it is straight and swift, it can still hold some pretty good fish. One or two or three qualities might not quite match the ideal, but there may be compensating factors. Remember what I said about Quicksilver Creek? The average year-round temperature of the water is 39 degrees, and the highest I ever recorded, on an August day when it was 92 in the shade, was 62 degrees. The stream's average daytime August temperature is 52 degrees. That's really too cold to be counted as perfect for trout, but it has natural and manmade advantages that soften the edges of its crackling coldness; plenty of bank vegetation, moderate velocity, and fertility that comes close to that of the Gunflint.

What I'm really talking about is a web. A first-class trout stream is an intricately woven web. One strand may be thin if another is thick enough to bear extra weight, but they all must achieve a balance. The presence of shade trees, bankbrush and pools where the sun's rays can penetrate to warm the bottom help moderate temperatures, and they're also connected to available food and energy output, bank stability, and hiding places. A web, an ecosystem, a closed circle . . . it helps when you can see it.

Something else to look for is the clarity of the water in a stream. When it is at normal levels, water clarity can tell you a great deal about fertility.

Extremely clear conditions, where you can see bottom distinctly in eight feet of water, and the stream doesn't seem to be there at all at hip depths, usually signal poor fishing. This kind of purity, while a delight to the eye, suggests a lean stream, short on life. To the extent that all living things pollute their environment, a truly unpolluted stream suggests sterility, and I have found that maxim to be reliable.

Generally, this class of stream will drain down from headlands of granite or basalt. Such streams are deceptive and terribly disappointing in that they often occur in wild places, where you suspect that the trout have never seen a hook, and the cold, crystal water helps to reinforce your conclusion. I once bushwhacked my way into such a place, drawn by its isolation and the magnetic though ironic ring of its name: Trout Brook. It was a nice place to visit, but I know you wouldn't want to fish there.

Fertility, on the other hand, will appear as cloudiness or milkiness. You won't be able to see bottom clearly in four to eight feet of water. This clouding is usually the result of microscopic organisms, especially algae. It occurs in response to a stream's natural fertility, and the same nutrients in the water that encourage these blooms work their way up in the food chain, until they reach the trout. Streams with these qualities commonly emerge as springs from, or drain headlands that are rich in calcium, especially limestone.

Sometimes cloudiness isn't all that apparent, either. Fertile water passing over riffles and bars may seem clear as glass. Quicksilver Creek, for example, appears ether-clear in the summer. Scoop a drink up in a glass, and except for a nymph or two, it is indistinguishable from tap water. But when you try to peer down into its deeper holes, the water develops a hazy bluish-green hue at around four feet.

There is an even better test if you think you've found the mother lode. Pick up a rock from the stream and examine its underside. Fertile streams crawl with subaquatic insect life.

The presence of aquatic vegetation is another sign of fertility and a coat of many colors. In its brightest shades, plants such as duckweed, sago, and watercress suggest stream velocities that are perfect for optimum trout growth rates. Vegetation also functions as an insect factory, feeding station, and sanctuary, and it helps keep the water cool.

However, excessive, unnatural fertility from some outside source such as agricultural fertilizers, industrial pollution, or improperly treated sewers, can ruin a stream by smothering it to death with plant life and algae blooms. The situation is aggravated even more with the introduction of thermal pollution, which is often the pool-ball result of the abnormal blossoming of plant life. It is a chain reaction that can suffocate the finest trout waters.

Stream width as a function of quality? Yes, I have found it to be so. There is a kind of optimum balance between water and bank, a demonstrable but difficult-to-define ratio between river frontage and surface square feet of water that I have found relates to fishing quality. I've always found the best fishing in streams that average less than 60 feet across. Granted, some of the big rivers around here are much wider than this, but the places I prefer to fish them are where they braid into islands and channels. Given this geography, bank-to-water ratios agree. Personal aesthetics play a part in this judgment, though. I just can't get as intimate with big water as I can on a stream where the periphery of my vision encompasses both banks and the water between. Fishing big rivers is not my strong suit. They are too impersonal and emotionally confusing.

Strangely enough, though, I enjoy fishing in lakes. I prefer them to be small, but even on a big lake, I can really get into working a shore, or an inlet stream, or a weed bank. It is a reflective pastime, more relaxing than stream fishing because you don't have to allow for moving water. The ingredients that suggest a good lake are about the same as those for a stream too, although some of those elements manifest themselves differently.

Stable banks with vegetation that meets the water, less-than-gin clarity, and temperatures in the summer that get no higher than 70 degrees two feet under the surface, are all favorable conditions.

So is considerable depth, but it must be balanced with shallows. A body of water with 30- to 40-foot holes virtually guarantees that trout can always find their tolerance level, no matter how hot the surface gets. The sun can't penetrate to these limits, and water behaves much like air: warm water rises and cold water sinks.

However, very deep water is, for all practical purposes, dead water as far as trout are concerned. A lake with a shore that plunges off into a pit can support a few fish, but very little of the sun's energy converts into food. In order for this conversion to take place, the sun must reach some part of a muddy or marly bottom, where it can foster the growth of aquatic vegetation, the first link in the food chain.

So long as there is a coldwater sanctuary present, the more fertile shallows a lake has, the more trout it will support.

This rule has one important exception however. In northern climates, and at very high altitudes, many fertile waters "freeze out." The term suggests a lake that turns into a colossal ice cube, but that is not the case. Ice remains on the surface of the lake for such a long period of time that rotting aquatic vegetation from the previous summer uses up all the oxygen. These lakes really "suffocate-out" and are incapable of supporting a population of trout.

Now let me ask you something. I have given you all the information you would need to find Gunflint Creek or the Goldfish Bowl, if you ever stumbled across them. It's really nothing more than a basic grasp of what makes a trout stream tick.

But how about this place? How does it look to you, how does it feel to you?

Good! And I would agree. It does appear to be a classic, and best of all, it's less than an hour's drive from home.

Have you noticed the fish rising downstream of the first meander? I thought so. You have good eyes, and you look at a river with your head. Well, let's get with it. Park the wagon, and let me take a quick look at the equipment you brought.

But first, we'd better consider that white sign tacked to the trunk of that big birch. I can't make out the small print, but the big letters are clear enough. This place is. . .

2 / "Posted" Signs and Other Crimes Against Nature

Without your having said a word, I can see we're thinking the same thing. Those selfish signs often spell the end of freelance angling, and I find them infuriating and ugly, a blight on troutfishing and a crime against nature . . . human nature. By their very presence they at once suggest and deny the possibility of exceptional fishing, and their mute insolence is cruel and ruthless.

My first reaction to a posted sign is to pretend I didn't see it, but the damn things are impossible to miss, and they loom larger and more formidable as you approach the boundaries they set. Tear them down? A fleeting dream of the triumph of justice. Property rights are the reality.

"The hell with property rights, I'll just sneak on by," you say? No, that won't work. You can't really catch a trout from the wrong side of the law because you keep looking over your shoulder instead of for the fish. Poaching is a denial of freedom, not an assertion of it. And even if you don't buy my ethical arguments, consider that the guy who put that sign up might be named Lothar and that his knuckles drag on the ground.

So it seems that we are shut down, at least here. But there must be other places to fish nearby, all you have to do is look. You know what to look for now, and that is a valuable talent. You are no longer bound by word of mouth, reputation, or trial-and-error. In a sense, you are much freer now than you were earlier, so our morning has hardly been wasted.

Realize too,. that posted signs do not automatically deny access. Their message takes many forms, often the opposite of what they seem to say. Even stern prohibitions like "No Hunitng, No Fishing, No Trespassing" may not mean that at all. And there are times when they don't mean a thing.

Some of the more progressive states have affirmed the public nature of streams over a certain width. You can enter them from a public access such as a bridge or a bordering highway, and wade or float them, so long as you don't get out on the bank. Most states recognize these rights on lakes, too.

Navigable waterways are another means of legal access. The term suggests the lower reaches of big rivers, industry, and barge traffic, but in fact, the status comes from the early days of logging when timber moved by water. Through one device or another, streams from rills that you could jump across to mighty rivers floated logs from timbercuts to mill. To prevent unscrupulous landowners or competing lumbermen from holding up timber traffic, virtually every waterway in timber country was declared navigable and open to public trespass up to the high-water mark. This is of considerable importance to us trout fishermen in that much timber country is still a wild preserve, though in private hands.

And don't forget, you can always ask for permission to fish. I've found that between one-half and three-fourths of the people who put up "Posted" signs will let you fish if you just ask. The signs are there, not as a proclamation of greed, but as one of exasperation. You can understand how landowners get tired of nameless intruders, of litter, and of being good guys only at their own expense.

Look at it this way. Even when you behave yourself as a perfect gentleman and sportsman, you will still take more than you leave. Whether or not you catch or keep a thing, your presence will have some effect; like trampled grass or broken branches, or perhaps you'll alarm a herd of cattle, which will lose three pounds of collective weight or a quart of collective milk as its runs the other way. Multiply that by two fishermen a day, seven days a week, and little things grow to mean a lot ... especially when you're a stranger.

Just introducing yourself will begin to break down a lot of the hostility behind a "Posted" sign. If you have a business card, leave one behind, pointing out that if anything is unsatisfactory after you leave you can be contacted at such-and-such a number. Ask the landowner if he'd like to have a trout or two, should luck be with you.

If you want to come back often, leave more than you take. That is the key to getting around "Posted" signs legally. Send Christmas cards. Bring an occasional jug of decent whiskey if your benefactor enjoys a drink. If not, a box of candy.

A more personal touch brings more personal contact. Dropping off a smoked trout ... on days when I didn't ask to fish ... has opened up iron curtains for me. So has collecting streamside and pasture litter, and repairing loose wires and broken gates. Once, when I was caught in the act, the farmer couldn't believe it at first, and then he told me that I had better be careful. If my practice caught on, he'd let *everyone* fish his stream, and then I'd have no trout left. He was kidding, but only about halfway.

There are also a few things not to do; discourtesies that are sure not to get you invited back. Don't call or show up at 5 A.M. ... or 11 P.M. ... and ask to go fishing. It is both rude and extraordinarily bad timing.

If your request for permission implies you'll be coming alone, don't bring your fishing buddies. In fact, it's bad form ever to show up with more than one friend.

If you have a yappy, face-licking, leg-humping mutt, for heaven's sake leave him home! He's bound to get into somebody's chickens or chase livestock, an act that will likely get him, and possibly you, shot. It will be justifiable homicide.

Don't litter. Not so much as a hank of discarded line. In fact, pick up any streamside garbage you see, especially if it is traceable to fishermen, because right or not, you will be held responsible. This is one reason why the otherwise noble craft of baitfishing has such a bad name in some circles. Baitfishing paraphernalia—hooks, sinkers, and worms—usually comes in throwaway containers, and some fools do just that. The flat, plastic packaging that holds commercial fly leader is another common candidate for bad public relations. In this case, at least, the "leave more than you take" attitude should work in the reverse.

What if there are no names to identify the landowner on a "Posted" sign, no way to get in touch with him quickly? That is a sign that the balance of fairness just might be off enough to register "tilt." If there's a uniform posting law in effect, you can probably legally ignore the message.

Uniform posting laws lay down specific requirements for the legal posting of land. They set minimum distances for the spacing of signs, and usually require that the person posting identify himself by name and address, and indicate annual renewal of the practice. For example, this may be accomplished by the simple act of crossing out the last year, and penning in the present one.

No, we don't have one in this state. I've been talking just that idea up at the trout club, and it's catching on, so maybe we might get something done through the legislature in a year or so. It is a necessary, fair, and equitable protection for landowner and sportsman alike. But even though I'd like to see it. I can't help but feel that the need for it is a little sad. Another reminder that times have changed.

Twenty years ago there was a sense of community around

here. Farmers and fishermen knew and respected each other, and they were mutually responsible for the consequences of their actions. Highways, jets, and lifestyles changed that, and now instead of an initial assumption of friendship between the two, it is one of antagonism. I will not suggest who is at fault, only that it is too easy for a person, soured on sportsmen, to tack up "Posted" signs all over the countryside that deny the pleasure of soft streams and the cool shade of trees without reason or right. Or for someone, more selfish yet, to reserve a public opportunity for their private interests. A "Posted" sign that reads nothing more than "keep out" is an infallible bluff. It also can be an unspeakable crime.

If a game law violator is a thief, then illegal posting is the act of forty thieves, because it denies at least that number of legitimate sportsmen the exercise of their pleasure. It is a little like white collar crime; you're safest if you steal millions instead of tens. It is a logic that escapes me, but one that is partially corrected by uniform posting.

What to do about an anonymous sign when there is no posting law? Well, your only recourse is a trip to the county seat. Land ownership is a matter of public record. Request the plats of the properties adjoining the stream in question and the authorities will tell you who owns what and where they live. Granted, it is an act of devotion to spend a day among musty archives when you could be fishing; but the possibilities of obtaining permission are excellent if you do. I have found that when landholders are really serious about refusing trespass, they usually identify themselves by name, brand, or corporation. Vague signs tacked up by legitimate landowners are measures designed to hold back "the public," that amorphous mass of humanity that migrates out from the cities. When you trace a landowner down and make personal contact, you move into another state of being, with a name, a face, an identity, and more often than not, permission to fish.

But posting can mean other things than a landowner who wants you to be more than a stranger on his property. That silent sign staring us down may be notice that this stream has been leased by a club. To my mind, this is the sorriest sign of all.

"Club" waters are worth asking about, just to make sure the club exists. There is a small chance that a club arrangement is a very loose agreement between property owners and "club" members . . . nothing more than a, "We'll take care of the posting, if you'll let us fish" relationship. In these situations, landowners can, and often do, grant other permissions. But clubs that sell memberships and lease land are locked up tight unless you join. Their "No trespassing" signs convert to notice that the stream is bought and paid for, and that money can catch a trout. On the level of fish-in-hand the conversion works, but in deeper, more abiding currents of thought, that kind of "club" fishing is less than ideal.

Don't get the impression that I'm down on all clubs. They have their place, and one is that if a bunch of guys want to get together, and post a little stocked pond . . . create an illusion of troutfishing in what would otherwise be barren water . . . I can see that. But there is something immoral about trading wild trout for cold cash. I can sympathize with a landowner who leases fishing rights or charges rod fees. He sees trout as a crop, and fees as some compensation for the annoyance of trespassers. But I cannot approve of the practice, nor would I participate in it. The public nature of game and fish was one of the things that made us special as a nation; a revolutionary idea 200 years ago, and paying for wild trout twists that principle around. It's really selling fish, an act that is contrary to the concept of sport.

Another problem is that leases and clubs often lead to supplemental stocking of waters that are capable of supporting a wild trout population. People join clubs because they want to have guaranteed fishing, and stocked trout represent the quickest means to that end. "What could be wrong with that?" you ask. "After all, it is a valid bargain, no different than buying meat. . . ."

Well, prepare yourself for a surprise. Stocking an otherwise "natural" stream is a damaging act because it eliminates wild fish, and eventually all fish, from the waters where it is practiced.

The heart of the problem lies in the conflicting nature of "tame" versus "wild" trout. The former are gregarious and ignorant, the latter, solitary, territorial, and wily. When a tame trout moves in on a wild trout, everything seems normal to the hatchery fish, but the wild trout does not want the company. This naturally-reared fish has learned to live in harmony with the world around him, to function within certain specific borders. The presence of a tame trout nearby is literally intolerable to a wild fish, so it leaves its accustomed lair, and, so displaced and disoriented, its chance for survival is seriously diminished.

But there has been an even greater loss than trading off tame for natural trout; hatchery fish have a notoriously low survival rate, no matter where they take up residence. Of 100 stocked fish, fewer than ten may be expected to survive after three months in waters where there is no fishing whatsoever! Hatchery fish thus displace and destroy wild trout populations, then self-destruct, and everyone is a loser.

Your reaction is predictable. Stocking as a means to boost catches is a measure that's deeply imprinted on American trout fishermen. I'll bet you demand it in public waters . . . that some percentage of your license fees be mandated to the raising and planting of "catchables." But the fact is that if that money were spent instead on improving stream habitat—stabilizing banks, correcting channelization damages, and anchoring headland soils in place, there would eventually be more trout in these streams. And of even greater significance than numbers, they would be quality fish. The miracle wouldn't occur overnight. I'd guess that the best you could hope for would be three to four years on a top-notch stream. Nature is a patient worker, and slow, but she is so much better than our feeble attempts to imitate her with the bland products of a hatchery pond, that she . . . and we . . . deserve it.

I am not suggesting that all public stocking is wrong. If there was never such a thing as put-and-take fishing in the little ponds of my boyhood, I probably never would have known or cared what a trout looked like. And I must admit that fishing for stocked trout, even today, is better than nothing. I've enjoyed that pleasant artificiality on public and private waters often. But stocked ponds or streams should be incapable of supporting viable natural populations.

And, although it was better to have fished stocked waters than not to have fished at all, in no way were these trout or their milieu comparable in vigor, vitality, or charm to the robust results of a wild environment. Substituting one for the other, when there is no good reason to do so, is yet another crime against nature.

Yes . . . there, he rose again, up against the bank. I've been watching that trout too. I think he knows he's safe, otherwise he wouldn't be so arrogant. There's a small hatch coming off. See the flies that have collected on your hubcap? That's what I meant about stream watching. We are both learning things, just standing on this bridge, and we can't fault the day. The sky is an infinite blue, and the sun is beginning to cut through the cool moistness of the morning. In another half an hour, we will call it hot. Some people would call this killing time, but what we are really doing is enriching it.

Talking about enrichment, there are those kind of clubs, too. I guess you could call them "public" clubs . . . I belong to one. They come together in small towns and large cities, and amount to a place where trout fishermen can pool their ideas and energies and accomplish something through the weight of their association and common interests. Things like stream restoration and improvement projects, cementing landowner relations, and leaning on the state legislature when the proposed widening of the shoulder of highway 191 threatens to elbow some trout out of the Marble River.

And there is a national association of trout fishermen too, called Trout Unlimited. That's another one I cast my lot with every year. You really should be a member if you aren't already. Their sole purpose is to maximize the opportunities for troutfishing, so you can only gain by joining. Here, let me write down their address:

It's twelve-and-a-half bucks well spent, and you get a quarterly magazine that articulates the problems and pleasures of trout and fishing far better than I can.

Which reminds me, we've gotten pretty far afield. But as I said, "Posted" signs can be very misleading things. I once kept driving by a patch of them for three months on my way to fish an unposted place 50 miles away. Then I finally got curious about all the people who were parking underneath them and read the signs. They said, "Park your car here and walk in," under the big, angry letters. So I did. Great fishing, too. Much better than the stream I'd been going to. So "Posted" signs can have a positive side.

There's one other possibility confronting us, though. Lately,

I've been seeing a lot of signs that read "Catch-and-release fishing," "Flyfishing," or "Trophy fishing only." I can imagine how you feel about these restrictions, but when I find them tacked to trees, I go someplace else.

You look surprised, and I can guess why. You've been told that returning fish to the water is better management of a resource, and that flyfishing is more sporting and less injurious to trout. Putting small trout back so they can grow up is another attitude that is deeply ingrained in American sporting ethics.

At first glance, these convictions seem so right, especially with the current thread of thought that suggests it's sinful to kill and eat a trout. But if you look behind the bushes, if you'll closely examine the reasoning behind these kinds of regulations, and the implications they hold for the future, you begin to wonder if they might not eventually destroy what they're supposed to preserve.

How? Okay, let's take catch-and-release fishing. That's the only policy that has provable merit, but catch-and-release fishing, in its essence, reflects a sense of offensive Platonism, an artifically enforced distance between you and your fish. The important word here is "enforced." I return better than half the trout I catch as a matter of habit, but as soon as it is required of me, the spell is broken. You can never really hunt with a camera, just as you can never really fish for a trout without the option of killing and eating him. It becomes affected drama, museum fishing, an incomplete circle that lacks an essential ingredient of satisfaction. I have fished catch-and-release waters at times, but I've never felt that I was really troutfishing; rather, just playing a game like football or baseball; and although these pastimes are called "sport," it is an unfortunate measure of the term. They are games. Sport is a very different matter; individual, final, and perfectly natural. To confuse the two destroys true sport.

"Quality" is the term I hear used most often in defense of catch-and-release regulations; that when you turn all your fish back to the stream, everyone catches more fish. The implication is that quality is defined purely by the numbers of trout you catch in a day. Sure, some of my most memorable days have been because of a big catch, but there are other factors that promote quality; solitude, a sense of discovery, freedom, effort expended and rewarded, and the exercise of independent thought, to name just a few. Catch-and-release fishing is like dropping a hook in an aquarium. It promotes mediocrity and a kind of academic distance between fish and fisherman. When you turn over all the stones, quality and artificiality become incompatible, especially where sport is concerned. If a river can't give up some of its fish, it can't stand fishing.

That says most of it.

Artificiality is part of my reluctance to accept the wisdom of "flyfishing only" waters, but I'm also concerned because they are a kind of monument to self-interest. When you peel off all the onion skins, there's no logical argument for them at the center, unless you view troutfishing as a class-structured enterprise. And if it is, why not "lure-fishing only" and "worm-fishing only" stretches of stream?

The reason most people give for wanting flyfishing exclusively is that it does the least damage to trout, so that they stand the best chance of survival when they're released. But it isn't true. The United States Fish and Wildlife Service did a study on the real damage different types of terminal tackle do to trout, and published it in *The Progressive Fish Culturist*. It was entitled, "The Hooking Mortality of Yellowstone Cutthroat Trout," and it indicated that there was no real difference in the damage done to a fish by barbed flies, barbless flies, barbed treble-hooked lures, barbless treble-hooked lures, and even bait-caught fish, so long as the bait was not swallowed. As a matter of fact, the lowest mortality rate was attributed to barbed treble-hooked lures. Only 2.7 percent of the fish caught on these lures died. The next "safest" bait was a barbless fly: 3.3 percent of the released trout died. The highest mortality rate, 73 percent, was among fish who swallowed a baited hook; but realize that the hook was always removed from the fish. I would place a sizable bet that the mortality of even bait-swallowing trout would be low if the fish were handled gently, the line were cut, and the hook allowed to remain inside the fish, where it would disintegrate naturally.

So what could be the real reason for "flyfishing only" waters? Frankly, I don't know. They are always crowded, loaded to the waterline with hatchery trout, and promoted to death.

More sporting? Sure, flyfishing has a reputation as the most sporting way to take a trout, but what are you suggesting? That worms or lures take unfair advantage? That they catch too many fish or catch them too easily?

I can only answer that from personal experience. I am neither a worm, nor lure nor fly fisherman, I am a trout fisherman. I use the tackle that conditions suggest is most appropriate at the time. I would guess that three-fourths of the trout I catch are taken on a fly. Without question, when I have one of those storybook days of a fish on every cast, it is when they are feeding on flies. And flies have proven to be the most effective type of tackle for about four-and-a-half months of a six-month season. If the relative success of a way of fishing is the issue, then perhaps it's flies that should be prohibited on some streams.

No, of course I'm not proposing something that silly, but you get the point. To tell you the truth, I'd much prefer to take a trout on a fly, but I'd never suggest to legislate what is really my personal taste, or impose it on someone else. Ultimately, that is nothing more than elitism, a form of discrimination, and an attack on civil liberties. Just like trout as they once were—the King's Game. And I find that prospect chilling, along with the assumption that anyone who fishes with a fly is a better person than a lure or worm fisherman.

We both know that some people are nicer than others; more gentle, more helpful, less selfish, more thoughtful, more genuinely concerned with others and their ideas, and with being a good sport. But I have not found the common denominator of these qualities to be the fishbait a person uses. Sportsmanship is more complex than that.

You seem confused. There are some questions that I can't answer, and explaining exactly what sportsmanship is, is one of them. Part of it grows from a love of the outdoors, and an intimate understanding of the clockwork of nature, and part of it involves a sense of fair play, but even there you can get into a confusion of values.

Take so-called "trophy fishing" regulations. They usually mean that you can keep fish over a certain size, around 16 to 18 inches, but you have to throw back the small-fry. What could be more sporting than that? This country has always been committed to protecting the underdog, the little guy.

But you can't compare people and wildlife. The natural pattern of things is to kill off a much greater proportion of young than old in any population of wildlife; including deer, ducks, rabbits and trout. When you are encouraged, and required by law, to remove only the biggest trout from a stream, the effect changes the age structure of trout populations.

See this triangle in the dust? A normal harvest of surplus fish, whether killed naturally or by fishermen, would create a triangle like this if you represented the numbers of fish by their age in a straight, black line. The longest, bottom line might be 1,000 fry, one-year old, the next line 800 3-inch trout, the next line 600 7-inch trout, and so forth, up to the very apex, which might represent five trout, five to seven years old, all 18 inches long or larger.

When you zero in on any one line, and hammer away at the fish that make it up, you are going to change the shape of the triangle. If you took nothing but small fish, there would be more big fish up toward the apex. But when you take nothing but so-called "trophy trout," you increase the broad base and end up catching nothing but bare "keepers."

And taking all the big trout you catch has implications beyond the mean size of resident fish. Lee Wulff has long argued that we should take the smallest trout, not the biggest and best of the species, as is common habit. His argument is that if we executed every man in America over six feet tall, over a period of time we would eventually eliminate that gene pool, and Americans would be smaller in structure than we are now. It is worth considering that we could be doing just that by killing large trout, and for what reason? They are certainly not the best eating, 8- to 12-inch trout are. And the "leave the little guy alone so he can grow up" is ill logic and contradictory to natural order. Don't succumb to the image that good fishermen bring home nothing but good fish. Killing a quality trout to bolster your image is one practice that I am sure has nothing to do with sportsmanship, yet it is encouraged by posting a stream for "trophy fishing only."

That is another ironic thing about limits of kind, size, or number; they set a goal you feel you must meet. They suggest you are obliged to take ten trout or six quail or five ducks. "Got my limit" is troutfishing's most dubious boast, but it's created and supported by the system.

Enough! . . . I've been watching him rise too. That fish is ready for the right fly. We might as well go and see who's posting this stream, and against what.

I know . . . you came to fish, and not to hear a lecture, but I hope you'll think about some of the things I've said. It makes no difference if we're posted-off these streams, legislated into senseless conformity, or if we lose it all because of our own greed and ignorance. The result will be the same; troutfishing will be diminished, and so will we.

Could you pull that branch out of the way so we can see the whole thing? Let's see, it says:

° POSTED °

The land behind this sign is private. Through an agreement with the owner, we have opened Back Brook to the public. Treat it as if it were your own. Respect the rights of others and the rules of sportsmanship. Leave more than you take, so others may continue to enjoy this privilege.

Signed, ✝

The Back Brook Sportsman's Assoc.

3 / The Premeditative Angler

Signs like that are a rarity these days; most of them are so negative and inhospitable. But look at its effect. It has turned the morning around for us, and created so much good will that the Salvation Army would be pressed to dispense with it all.

In addition to their sign of hospitality, the Back Brook Sportsman's Association has also provided a graveled parking area, a 55-gallon oil drum with the legend "Pitch In," and a wood-runged style that serves to protect the condition of your waders, and the barbed wire fence it straddles. Grassroots goodness. And look at your reaction to it. You will be more conscious than ever not to damage or abuse the trust it implies. A perfect attitude to accent a day of troutfishing.

Before we get on the stream, I'm interested to know what you brought by way of equipment. By the looks of the gear you've got laid out on the tailgate, I would say you're prepared for one kind of fishing. I don't know why, but it's more than rare to find a

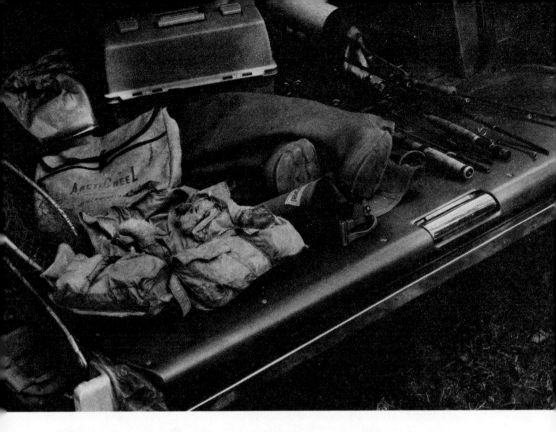

Renaissance trout fisherman these days; someone who knows how to use flies, lures, and bait, and who appreciates the charms and challenges of each. It's puzzling because flies, lures, and natural bait are complementary, not mutually exclusive. What you learn in the pursuit of one teaches things about the others. There is also the plain matter of catching more fish. There will be times when trout are so mad for flies that they will look at nothing else, and other times when worms are the only terminal tackle that will take fish. If you are not able to adapt to these changes in feeding patterns, you're missing a lot of action, and denying trout-nature.

Tell you what. Instead of criticizing your tackle box, let me show you what I've brought. I'll identify what can be bought by brand name, just in case you might want to duplicate it someday, but a mirror image of my tackle is not nearly so important as understanding why I choose a specific tool, and its function in the scheme of trout-and-stream.

I own four rods; one fly rod, two spinning rods, and what amounts to a combination fly/spin rod.

My fly rod is an 8-foot graphite six-weight, custom-built on a Lamiglass shaft. I cannot praise graphite highly enough for fly-casting. It is far more adaptable in the weight and tapers of line it will throw than glass or cane, and more powerful than either. I used to agonize over dry-fly and wet-fly actions, 8½-foot rods for big water, and matching up systems four through seven. This rod will handle it all reasonably well. Granted, it is not the exacting tool that a rod perfectly matched to line and action is; you always lose something when you move away from precision and toward generality. But its adaptability is a big plus for my brand of fishing, and a savings in cash and the sanity derived from simple decisions. If I had continued to support the habits of matched fly rods and owning every new development in the tackle industry, my soul would belong to the credit department of the Marble River Sports Shop.

Another influence on my reasoning was the gradual recognition that the quality and extent of the tackle you own plays a much smaller part in catching a trout than competence and understanding. It's difficult to reduce this to formulas, but I'm talking about things like the difference between a 15-dollar rod and a 500-dollar rod. There's a difference, to be sure, but in the hands of someone who knows how to use both rods, the 500-dollar rod would catch five or ten percent more fish than the 15-dollar rod.

The same parallels could be drawn between a knowledgeable trout fisherman who owns just one rod and carries a hip pocket full of equipment and a tackle collector who has a closet filled with the latest of everything, but doesn't really know how to use it. The good fisherman will outfish the tackle collector every time. I would go so far as to say that competence and understanding represent about 90 percent of what it takes to catch a trout, so make them your top priorities, not sophisticated or extensive tackle that is beyond need and understanding.

This is the rod I love to use on small streams, and in a way, it is my favorite; a Leonard LSF 56 UL, 5½-foot, glass-ferruled, ultra-lite spinning rod. It is short, light, and capable of double duty. It has an adjustable reel seat. With the seat removed to the end of the butt, and a fly reel mounted there, it is a perfect "flea rod" for small stream flyfishing. Move the reel seat midway up the cork grip, mount a 4-ounce spinning reel, and you are ready to fish tiny lures or bait over the same water.

The basis of this kind of adaptability, aside from the adjustable reel seat, lies in the shaft's parabolic action. Given a small measure of inaccuracy, a parabolic action defines the fly rod. It can be identified by placing the rod under stress . . . resting the tip on the floor and the butt in your hand. When bent, parabolic rods describe a curve that flows slow and smooth from the butt, then gradually arcs into a more radical curve as it reaches the tip.

Although parabolic actions are commonly thought of as fly

actions alone, they hold two important and largely unrecognized places in spinning. Ultralite rods should be parabolic rods because a shaft that "bends to the corks" helps compensate for the minuscule resistance set up by dime-weight lures and baits. Parabolic actions drive very light terminal tackle farther and with greater accuracy than "fast" actions.

Parabolic or "soft" actions are also perfectly suited to fishing with natural bait. Their nature is to slowly accelerate during a cast, an important contrast with fast rods, which snap like a whip. This gradual acceleration helps keep soft, live bait intact.

Which brings us to my bait rod. I use a Leonard LES 70 M, 7-foot glass-ferruled parabolic spinning rod. Parabolic spinning rods are extremely difficult to find in greater than ultralite lengths, as virtually all manufacturers have climbed on the fast-tip bandwagon, so this rod amounts to something of a treasure too. Before I discovered this one I used to build my bait rods on fly rod shafts, which is one option you might consider should a commercial bait rod prove impossible to locate. If I had my druthers, I would prefer a slightly longer shaft . . . 7½ or 8 feet . . . because to present it with maximum appeal, a bait must drift naturally, and a long shaft increases your line's angle of incidence to the water. This, in turn, reduces current drag and its effect, affording a drift that follows natural lines of flow. But this shaft has exquisite baitfishing qualities and a sensitivity that I've never been able to duplicate with a converted fly rod, so I stick with it.

For lure fishing I use a Fenwick FS70, 7-foot, fast-taper, glass-ferruled spinning rod. This is a rod suited to large ¼- to ⅝-ounce spinning lures on big streams, rivers, and lakes. "Fast tip," "omni," or "universal" action in a rod is defined by a radical taper or step-down in shaft diameter somewhere in the tip section. The closer that step-down is to the tip, the "faster" the rod. The performance derived from this feature finds the tip section capable of driving comparatively light spinning lures with an effortless flick of the wrist. When the rod is stressed by a heavy fish, the bulky butt section goes to work cushioning the shock of runs and dives; the more powerful they are, the closer the bend moves to the butt. Fast-tip action may be identified in the same way as are parabolic actions: by resting the tip on the floor and the butt in your hand. A fast action will exhibit a sharp bend at the point of the taper, as opposed to a smooth, progressive curve.

I carry all four of my rods in individual cloth cases, housed inside this 4-foot section of 6-inch diameter plastic PVC sewer pipe, with a solid fitting on one end, and a screw cap on the other. You can locate these parts in any plumbing supply store.

The reels I use reflect the same diversity that I expect of my rods. For flycasting I use a Hardy Princess fly reel, with three arbors. A Hardy is a bit of an extravagance for me, but it was a gift from a good and true fishing partner that I have come to treasure. There is a comfortable excellence in its smooth performance that feels good to hold. And it has the most elegant ratchet in the world; it doesn't scream, it whispers.

My arbors hold three different lines, all made by Scientific Anglers; a double-taper six-weight floating line, a weight-forward taper seven-weight floating line, and a weight-forward taper seven-weight floating line with a high density sinking tip. I always carry the sinking tip line, but sometimes leave the floating line in my tackle box in the car. On small streams I carry the double taper. On lakes and large rivers, I carry the weight-forward taper.

For spinning on small streams, I carry a Cardinal "3" ultralite reel, with two spools, one loaded with 4-pound test, one loaded with 2-pound test. With it, the Leonard ultralite rod, and the Hardy fly reel holding double-taper floating line, I am in heaven on Quicksilver Creek, able to meet virtually any condition that arises after a 2-minute switch of reels.

For bait and lure fishing on big waters, I use a Cardinal "4" medium weight spinning reel with two spools, one loaded with 6-pound test Trilene and one with 8-pound test high-visibility yellow Stren. I favor the Cardinal brand reels because they are as quiet as a still night, reasonably priced, and have proven to be trouble-free. They also incorporate two features I have come to demand in my spinning reels; pushbutton spool changing, and a drag adjustment in the rear of the reel body, where it is easy to get at when you are fighting a fish. I use this medium-weight reel in conjunction with two spinning rods, the Leonard bait rod and the Fenwick lure rod. I use the 6-pound test line for lures, and the 8-pound test high-visibility line for bait. When you are fishing bait, being able to see exactly where the line enters the water is part of the trick, so this stuff is a tremendous fishing aid. I suspect that fish can see this line in clearish water, so when these conditions prevail, I use a short, conventionally-colored leader.

As you can see, I carry these reels in the bottom compartment of a 16" by 10" by 9" Adventurer 1999 tackle box, with each reel protected by an old sock. The extra spools and arbors go there too, with similar protection.

Here is the best investment you will ever make—a pair of Royal Red Ball Cahill chest waders. They are as essential to trout fishing as a hook and line. Whatever terminal tackle you're using, getting to the right position in a stream to work the fish is always your guiding star. Hip waders always seem to be 2 inches too short to get into position or to cross a creek, or to clear a backcast. Chest waders open up highways of water for 60 bucks, and I like Royal Red Ball best for two reasons. It has a tailored fit so my stride isn't snapped off when I step up, and it keeps water out one season longer than every other make I've tried. If you wade in cold water, it can be bought with an insulated boot. You trade walking weight for warmth, but the exchange is worth it. Another worthwhile sacrifice; take 15 minutes to cover the boot-soles with indoor/outdoor carpeting. It takes the slide out of those greased cannonballs that pave the beds of swift streams.

This is a personal favorite too, and getting a little tattered around the edges from use: a home-sewn ripstop nylon fishing vest. It was a birthday present from my wife Sil. The ribcage design gets back to the stream position thing . . . with it, I can wade deep without getting my flies wet. And it has a lot of room to stow boxes and bottles; two large and six small pockets in front, and one very large pocket in back. The lambswool fronting on the two breast pockets is great when you want to change flies in a hurry and don't want to drag out another box. The material is important too. I like ripstop nylon because it takes up little packing space. This vest often serves as my "tackle box" when I'm traveling or backpacking.

When the vest is on my back I may use it for fly, lure or baitfishing gear, but I switch its contents according to what the fish want that day.

This 12-inch aluminum net is an essential too. Not just for landing fish, but for releasing them. The factors most likely to damage fish are prolonged battles and rough handling. When you don't use a net, the fish is usually played out by the time you slip your hand around his middle, and half the time it wriggles free to fight some more. Critical energy is preserved via a quick scoop, and the trout is much easier to handle inside the net. The mesh affords greater purchase than a bare hand, too, so you don't have to squeeze hard to immobilize the fish; and the mesh also helps keep the fishskin wet and the slime intact. Ironically, not wearing a net has become something of a badge among some fishermen; a symbol that they keep no trout. They might not keep any, but by this practice, they are still responsible for killing a few.

A net also gives you a better opportunity to assess a trout's condition. If you ever see bleeding from the gills, kill and keep him. His chances for survival are near zero.

This canvas Arctic Creel and my aluminum net represent a compromise of my aesthetic values. I wore an old, wicker creel and a graceful teardrop wooden net for years. They were badges of a sort, a statement of style that was pleasing to look at and felt good draped around you. But both always seemed in need of repair, and the boxy creel often got in the way of a cast or fighting fish. A side-hugging, flat canvas creel doesn't create that problem, and wetted canvas is a far more effective coolant than wicker, fern, and grass. But it's still not as pretty to look at in 10 o'clock sunlight as the golden geometric wickerwork, the damp, green ferns, and a brace of fat brook trout . . .

Let me empty some of this stuff out so you can see it better. Quite a pile of junk, huh? I'll bet you never thought so much could be crammed into such a small space. But it's all going to fit back . . . I think. Hand me that vest. We'll sort out the fly tackle first.

These Worth 9-foot 6X leaders, with a 2-pound tippet, are my standard. I prefer tapered, knotless leaders because knotted leaders tend to tangle when the fly rolls over and knot rubs against knot on the leader. This is especially true when casting in a cross wind. I am a natural expert at tying accidental "wind knots" already, and I don't need any more help.

I do not always fish these leaders at factory lengths, however. I use long, light leaders only when the water is extraordinarily clear. I make it a practice to use the heaviest tippet that seems practical, given the water conditions and sophistication of the trout, and will occasionally use 8-pound tippets if I can get away with it. This is considered dirty pool in some quarters, but I have my reasons. First, I like to feel a fish work. I enjoy a brief one-on-one battle that is over in minutes much more than an endless see-saw give-and-take exchange of line. I find no pleasures in the howl of a ratchet, but it sure feels good when a heavy fish is pressured and pumping in my hand. It brings out the best in him, and in me. Heavy leaders, maximum-pressure battles, and confrontations of short duration are also kinder to the fish. He comes to net less exhausted, and quicker to recover when you release him.

Try as I may, I cannot understand the logic behind the school of thought that holds that to catch very large fish on very light tackle is the essence of sportsmanship. The perfection of modern tackle and drag systems makes such battles more of an exercise than an excitement, and I speak as one who has caught an 125-pound sailfish on 14-pound fly tackle . . . and who doesn't care to do it again.

This Nylorfi leader material goes into one small front pocket of my fishing vest. I carry 25-meter rolls of 8, 6, 4, and 2-pound leaders, connected by a short length of string which passes through the hole in the middle of each spool, and holds the four rolls together. Leader material can then be stripped off the rolls like line from a multiplying reel, and they stay together in an easy-to-grab package. As fly changes and losses eat up my original leader, I blood-knot the necessary additional leader material to the end. In this way, two or three commercial knotless leaders last for a whole season.

Seidel "600" leader sink fits in the next small pocket. I do not use it as a matter of course, only when I'm dry-flyfishing over clear, slow-moving streams and lakes, and then I only apply it to the last 12 inches of the tippet. A sunken leader drags a fly down with it, and fish won't pick out a floating leader when the surface pane is broken by current agitation. On the other hand, when the pane is glassy, even a 6X tippet casts a shadow like a hawser when it is floating because the surface tension that holds it above water bends light. As I said before, I don't use it often, but when leader sink is called for, it is indispensable.

Garcia Silicote dry-fly dressing, Seidel's "800" dry-fly powder, and a Kleenex tissue reside in the same pocket as the leader sink. When I first dress a dry, I use the Silicote. After its effect wears off, I squeeze the fly in the tissue and apply the powder. It is the best way I know to keep a dry-fly floating, and its effectiveness finds testimony in the fact that I am a terrible fly-tyer. Even my hair flies sink like a stone without this stuff, unless, of course, I'm fishing a hair streamer like the Muddler. Then they float like a cork.

A vial of BB-sized Water Gremlin shot goes in the third small pocket. I prefer this brand because the "jaws" in the rear of the shot make it easy to remove. I occasionally use these weights to correct my floating Muddlers, and for some nymph fishing. There are days when the trout insist on an unweighted nymph that hovers just off the bottom.

The extra Hardy arbor fits in the last of the lower pockets; it is virtually always the one holding the high-density sink-tip line.

One of my breast pockets contains this 2-foot-square chunk of cheesecloth. Stretched between two willow twigs, it makes an acceptable and instant seine to help identify what underwater life the trout might be dining on. It has also served me as emergency bandage material, towel, and handkerchief. I never remember to take a handkerchief when I go fishing.

This other small breast pocket is open for incidentals . . . a roll of film, pack of smokes, a hockey puck, or whatever. I do not carry scissors or hemostats. It is their nature to dingle or dangle from a vest, and I'm always snapping them with fly line on a forward cast. I do, however, carry a Swiss Army pocketknife from Precise Imports Company, which has a scissors blade, and two cutting blades, Phillips and standard-head screwdriver blades, a file, and an awl. I cannot speak highly enough of this tool as a medium of streamside repair, or begin to recall the number of times it has salvaged a fishing trip.

The two large front pockets of my vest house my files. Dries are kept in a Perrine aluminum box with multiple holes for air circulation, and spring-loaded slots that lock the hooks in place and the fly in an upright position. Hackles get a little flat, but it holds a far greater number of flies with less volume than do individual plastic boxes.

I keep my small nymphs in a Scientific Angler's fly box, with longitudinal spring-plastic slits, into which the bend and barb of the hook fits. The flies are snug, and they are easy to identify, remove, and replace.

I keep large, fuzzy nymphs, and fluffly deer-hair minnows in this six-compartmented, divided Cortland unbreakable fly box. Wets and streamers and bucktails that can be stored flat go into this little wallet with sponge rubber leaves, called a "Tackle Tote."

I tie my own flies, so I can afford to carry quite a few. Have you ever tried it, or rod building? If you haven't you really should. It's a great excuse to avoid company you really don't want to see, and work you'd rather not do, as well as an inexpensive way to supply what has become a very expensive class of trout tackle, especially if you're also a hunter, because you can harvest about a third of the required feathers and hairs while pursuing that pastime. But beyond cold cash, there is a kind of sublime integrity about catching a fish on your own creation (another ripple ringing out), and when you can tie a fly, you are then capable of independent direction. You start doing things like bringing home mayflies in bottles, and playing God. One of the most satisfying successes in fishing is to take a trout on your interpretation of the universe, and whether it is ratty, a sinking-floater, or a floating-sinker, doesn't seem to make a hell-of-a-lot of difference to the fish once you've built what they're after.

I thought you'd do a doubletake when the box sprung open. There's quite a few there, about 120. But look at the patterns, and the numbers of flies that are all the same, just different sizes. Although I'm a serious experimenter, the patterns belie my success. In descending order of numbers, I have Royal Coachmen, Light Cahills, Adams, Goofus Bugs, Bivisibles, Quill Gordons, Joe's Hoppers, Mosquitoes, and Raiders. The rest of my dries are mainly experimental ties that have worked about a quarter of the time, but each was made in response to a specific, selective hatch. When there is nothing to suggest selectivity, I invariably gravitate toward the old standards. I would say that 80 percent of the trout I take on dries fall to one of these established patterns, and about 40 percent are caught on either the Royal Coachman or Light Cahill.

These are my nymphs, about 100 of them. You can see I have Wooly Worms up the gazoo, especially in insect green, olive green, black, and brown. Hare's Ears are another prominent pattern, followed by Montana Nymphs. One of my major experimental successes looms next, an unnamed nymph. Let's call it a Hodges . . . he was a good friend and fisherman. It has taken trout wherever I fish it. It consists of nothing more than a black silk abdomen, wound with palmer-style grizzly hackle, and a dubbed, natural wool thorax on #16 and #18 hooks.

A Red Ant variation that strongly resembles a wingless Coachman comes next, and the rest of the nymphs are personal experiments again . . . with an awful lot of semi-successful attempts at caddis worms.

My streamers number 36. I am not a particular fan of fishing streamers or wets. Muddler patterns predominate, followed by Spuddlers, Spruce, Royal Coachmen and Mickey Finns. These dozen-odd patterns were mostly given to me by friends.

My wet selection—mainly Royal Coachmen, Leadwing Coachmen, and Black Gnats—is just as sparse as my streamer array. I also have bright Parmachene Belles and Silver Doctors, testimony to my infatuation with pansize beaver-pond brook trout. Their number comes to about forty.

The collective weight of the patterns I stock is derived from experience. When a particular fly performs well, I tie a lot of them. When a noble experiment has marginal success, I'll carry one or two. When a pattern, fanciful or traditional, doesn't seem to work, the hook gets rusty and I eventually discard the fly. This sort of natural selection suggests several things about trout and the flies they favor. First, old, popular patterns like the Royal Coachman still pack plenty of appeal, even in this day of match-the-hatch and Latin scholarship. Second, nondistinctive patterns, such as Light Cahills, Wooly Worms, and Hare's Ears, that may be taken for several types of real insects, are an essential reserve. There have been many times when I had what appeared to be just the right match to a hatch, but it didn't convince the fish. Something like a brown Wooly Worm had no relationship to what they appeared to be taking, but it caught trout. Finally, I have not enjoyed spectacular success with distinctive patterns designed to mirror specific life forms. I have a hunch that eye-catching touches like woven and segmented bodies, custom-blended furs, and sculptured wings hook more fishermen than fish. And trying to stock them all in one vest is a financial and practical impossibility, since their numbers are nearly limitless.

Now, let's see if I can get it all back in. Actually, I used to carry even more gear than this, but there's a point where planning for every possibility gets a little absurd. Every time I think that maybe I should have just one more fly box, or some little fishing gadget, I remember what the late Chris LoCascio said to me one day.

He used to run the Fisherman's Paradise Tackle Shop, and I hope he made it to the place from which he derived his store's name. It was a musty, fishy cornucopia of seductive equipment, and, to a 15-year-old trout addict, each piece on display represented an essential part of the complete angler. Just about every dime I had was spent there, and to achieving that end.

Then, late one Saturday morning, and adorned with less than half the gear I deemed necessary to confront a trout on his own terms, I stopped in the store to buy some lures.

Chris looked over the half-moons of his reading glasses at my fedora and its lambswool band, bristling with flies; my vest bulging with boxes and festooned with lures, scissors, and thermometer, my net, my oversized wicker creel stuffed with more boxes and no trout, my belt that held up my hip boots, a worm box, a lure box, and a floating, waterproof flashlight, and the harnesses on my felt creepers.

He was not, by nature, a profane man, but he understood the value of the right word at the right time. "Kid," he chuckled, "all you need is a broomstick up your ass, and you could sweep the floor too."

There ... I told you it would fit. Now pass me the tackle box and I'll sort out my spin gear. As you can see, it's about as complete as my fly gear, but I don't bring all these lures when I'm spinfishing. A lot of them are duplicates ... backup lures in case I lose a few. And too many of them are failures. I have this habit of buying every new lure I see in hopes that one will turn out to be a better mousetrap, but they seldom do, and I can't bring myself to throw them away.

As a rule, I end up selecting old standards that cover a fair representation of colors, weights, and actions, and I pack them in those two plastic boxes in the bottom of the tackle box. One box holds my ultralite lures, and the other, my standard-weight lures, and both of them fit into the two large pockets on my vest. That leaves me a lot of room to spare in the smaller pockets, and in those I put my bait paraphernalia.

Now the lures I plan to take today: two #0 Mepps and two #2 Mepps spinners with silver and gold blades; one #2 Mepps Fury with a black and yellow blade; one #1 Mepps Kris spoon with a blue blade, one #1 Mepps Aglia Long with a pearlized finish.

Three Dardevle "Spinnies," ¼-ounce, in nickel, brass, and pearlized finishes.

Two Wonderlures, ⅜-ounce, in gold- and silver-plated hammered brass.

Two Luhr Jensen Krocodiles, ⅜-ounce, in pearlized and brass finishes.

Six #1, #4, and #6 Panther Martins, ⅛-ounce, ¼-ounce, and ⅜-ounce, respectively, in silver and gold blades and bodies. Four #4 Panther Martins with silver and gold blades and black-and-yellow and red-and-yellow bodies.

Two Thomas Cyclones, 1/6- and ⅜-ounce, in hammered copper and silver. One Thomas Buoyant, ⅜-ounce, in silver.

One Kamlooper spoon, ⅜-ounce, in gold.

Two Fighting Fish, ¼-ounce, in gold and silver.

Two ¼-ounce Doty Raiders, in gold and silver.

Two Castmasters, in gold and silver, both ⅜-ounce.

Four Rapala #5 floating and sinking minnow plugs, in silver and gold, with black backs; and a dozen ball-bearing type snap swivels in the smallest size made.

When fishing large rivers, I also carry a few ⅝-ounce spoons and spinners, especially Kamloopers, Mepps, and Wonderlures. Lures under ⅜-ounce go in the ultralite box, those that are ⅜-ounce and up go in the standard spinning box.

And that's it. Like I said, streamlined. Lure fishing has its own kind of purity, and for that matter, so does baitfishing.

You can meet the demands of baitfishing in part, with the same cheesecloth I use to sample what might be floating down in the current. It can be used to seine bait, to catch minnows, or to pin a lively grasshopper or cricket to the ground. Other equipment I carry includes a bait box. An old Prince Albert tobacco tin is the greatest. Today, it practically rates as an antique, but it's ideal. You can substitute a tin Band-Aid box, or a telescoping plastic cigarette case, but these alternatives lack class. What all three containers have in common is that they will fit snugly in the breast pocket of my fishing vest, a far handier arrangement than a baitbox that you wear on your belt, especially when you're wearing chest waders.

I also have two small plastic boxes for hooks. One holds #4, #8, #10, and #12 Eagle Claw unsnelled baitholder hooks, a half-dozen of each. The other holds Mustad Universal Double Bait hooks in sizes #6 and #4, also a half-dozen of each.

Three plastic bags of Water Gremlin split shot: BB, #14, and cannonball size, make for casting weight and fast-sinking bait. This selection affords the latitude to match whatever current conditions you encounter. Again, I prefer this brand because it incorporates "jaws" in the rear of the shot which make it easy to change weighting, a persistent necessity owing to changing bottom conditions and water velocities.

A Spincaster clear plastic casting bubble. Notice how these floats are shaped a little like a bomb, with a lot of weight forward and a slim, tapered tail? They also incorporate spring-loaded line clips, so that they can be snapped onto your line without breaking off and retying. Their design makes for minimum wind and water resistance, and efficient casting.

Into the last pocket goes the extra high-visibility line spool, and the vest is then ready for spinning.

Depending upon the type of equipment I'm fishing, I store the unwanted tackle in the big tackle box. This is a far more flexible selection of gear than might be evident with it now laid out here before us in such neat order. By using the space inside the front pocket of the waders, and the extra pocket on the side of the creel, it's possible to tote *all* the terminal tackle, and an extra reel—a real advantage when a stretch of water waits a mile from the car. That's why I like that little Leonard so much; it keeps all my options open.

And that's it. I have a few extra rods and reels at home . . . things that I've collected over the years . . . but they're nothing more than backup equipment in case I have a breakdown, or someone wants to borrow a rod. Otherwise, this is the sum of my trout tackle; all that I've found I'll need.

The paper bag? That's not exactly fishing gear inside, it's lunch.

Tell you what; why not just use my tackle today? I don't mind watching instead of fishing, and the stuff you've brought is a little limited. Believe it or not, as much as I love catching a trout, it's almost as much fun to watch someone else do it, so long as you feel you're part of it. The real challenge of troutfishing for me is to look at and feel what's happening in a stream or a pond, interpret its condition, and come up with the way that will fool the fish. Who catches it isn't that important. So pull on your waders and let's take a closer look at Back Brook.

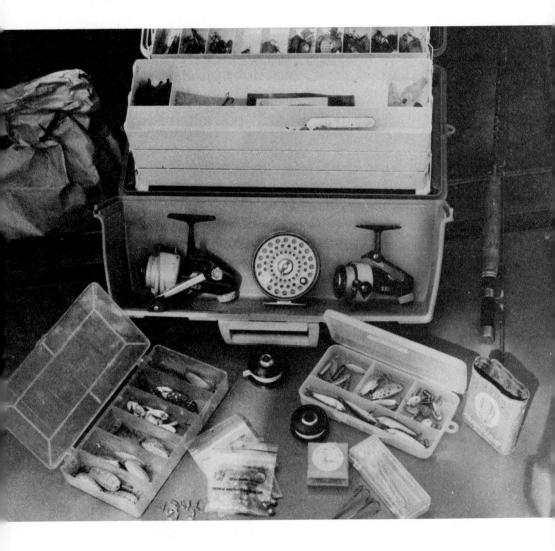

4 / *Reflections on a Trout Stream*

Stand in the stream, wade deep ... until you feel the rubber relent to the pressure and crinkle around your legs. There is always an unfamiliar sense of buoyancy and freedom when you first enter a stream, as if you could jump and float for a while before coming down. The moonwalk. The Great American Daydream.

It will pass given a few moments adjustment, but for now, go ahead and indulge yourself with its effect, letting one foot drift upward, then shifting weight to temporarily liberate the other. You've been here before, and so have I, but the sensation is no less otherworldly. We enter life through water, and according to people who should know, we once crawled our way out of the sea. Perhaps we're just coming home.

"In the water." That's John Silver's pleasure. He likes to catch a trout while he is in the water, and it's understandable. It brings the two of you closer together, puts you on more equal footing. I like boats for that reason too. Wading, boat fishing; you are so much more in tune than when fishing from the bank.

Feel Back Brook nudge you? It's name isn't really important. It could be the Alph or the Styx or the Hassayampa, or a river or a pond or a lake. Nor is its location essential. Back Brook is really a set of principles, but it yields a good catch nonetheless.

It is here where our fishing begins, standing in the water with empty hands, careful eyes, and a mind full of possibilities. The painter has his oils, the mathematician his numbers. When you are out to catch a trout, you start with the look and the feel of the water.

Back Brook, a beautiful little place. Complex, but ultimately no more than the sum of its parts. Things like velocity, bottom contours, bank conformation, clarity, temperature . . . When you look at those parts separately, you learn a lot about what the trout who live there might want, which, in turn, defines the tackle to use.

Take the time of day. Nothing more than a watch will give you a place to start. Early morning is usually the time to use bait. Beetles, spiders, slugs, and worms move around in the night and they thrive in the damp bottms along streams. Many of them fall into the water, and trout are attuned to this influx of food at first light.

Baitfishing time lasts from daybreak until the sun rises to 45 degrees off the horizon . . . when this happens, the shadows cast by objects will be equal to their height. Then lures enter the picture. What bait the night brought will have gone from the stream, and aquatic insects aren't yet active. Small fish now constitute the most evident and available meal.

Artificial flies usually produce best from one hour after the sun has reached its zenith, until dark. This period represents the time when waters are at their warmest levels during a 24-hour period. Like a garden, insect life blooms in the heat of the afternoon, and trout respond by turning their heads in that direction.

Temperature is another yardstick of feeding preferences. It can be gauged with a thermometer, but my soul says the instrument is a little too clinical. Use your hands. It's more satisfying.

If the water is below 45 degrees, it will feel numbing to your hand after 30 seconds, and it will begin to numb your throat if you drink it. This is one indication that trout will be looking for bait. Below-45-degree water will also become uncomfortable against your boots unless you're wearing insulated underwear.

Water that's between 45 and 55 degrees will feel cold on your hands, but they won't numb fast. It is pleasant to drink . . . just the right temperature for a hot day. It will chill your legs after you've been in the water for a while, but it won't feel uncomfortable. This temperature range suggests that you should use lures.

Water that is over 55 degrees may feel cold to the touch at first, but after 10 seconds or so, it won't be uncomfortable. If you are standing in the shade, and a light breeze is blowing, pull your hand from the water and let it start to dry. When you put it back in, the water will feel warmer than the air. The temperature range these tests indicate points toward flies as a probable favorite.

For all the precision suggested by specific numbers, however, you will find as many exceptions. It seems the temperature/food preference relationship depends on average temperatures, and average temperature spreads. For example, Quicksilver Creek is unusually cold. Waters hovering around 50 degrees represent the higher end of its seasonal temperatures. Fish look for flies at this time. In Limestone Spring Creek, a watercress-lined brooklet that emerges from the ground at around 52 degrees, water temperatures colder than 52 degrees downstream from its source signal sluggish trout that are likely to respond most readily to bait. So balance your judgment against average stream temperatures as well as you can determine them, remembering that the basic relationship will still hold true: cold-cool-warm suggests bait-lures-flies, in that order.

You should also consider water clarity in this loose equation, because it too, adds tones and hues to the picture these surroundings are painting. When the water is up to your calves and you can't see bottom I call it dirty. If my foot disappears when I wade up to my knees, it's roily. When I can see my foot in water around midthigh depths, I would call it milky, and when the features of the bottom are distinct, and the water is up around my waist or deeper, I call it clear.

Each of these conditions suggests a corresponding technique. Roily to dirty water practically dictates bait, no matter the time of day or temperature of the water. Dirty water results either from spring runoff or heavy rains upstream. The increase in water volume carried by a swollen stream kicks up velocities and the effect washes a lot of food into the water; banks cave in, riverbed rocks roll around . . . the water becomes loaded with nymphs, worms, ants . . . you name it.

Although this condition might seem to suggest that trout will take an artificial nymph, ant, or similar fly, you'll find that imitations are a poor second to the appeal of natural bait when streams are high and dirty. Artificials lack one essential ingredient at this time: odor. When trout can't see beyond their noses, they rely on these, rather than their eyes, to locate and identify food.

The progress of one awesome insect hatch, and the comparative productivity of artificials and live bait, is the best evidence I've run into for this change in feeding patterns.

Did you ever fish the giant stonefly hatch out West? That is some fishing! But it's not just the numbers and size of the trout you take, it's being there to see it happen. Enormous stoneflies, some as big as dragonflies, with 2-inch bodies and 3-inch wingspans, begin to emerge in late May and early June. They are timed to the Rockies' great leap into summer. It's as if the energy of the earth has been suppressed too long by the raw, cold spring in the high country. Grass grows inches a day, trees burst from bare branches to full leaf in a week, brown prairie turns into a carpet of wildflowers, and rivers swell with life and power.

About two weeks before this natural explosion, the nymphal stage of the fly leaves the nooks and crannies of the riverbed, and starts to move out toward the banks. In order to hatch into adults, the flies must first crawl onto tall grasses or bankwillows, where their exoskeleton can dry and crack in the sun and air. You can imagine how the trout react. Calling it a feeding orgy is an understatement.

But here's the interesting thing. At the start of the flies' movement toward the banks, rivers are usually milky-to-roily. The full fury of runoff hasn't flushed down from the mountains. The best bait for a trout at this time is an artificial fly, a big, salmon-pink-and-brown Stonefly Nymph, tied on a #6 long-shanked hook. It will outfish natural bait two-to-one, mainly because it is easier to dress, less time-consuming to fish, and less likely to snag on the bottom.

But as soon as the water turns dirty and the peak runoff hits, the effectiveness of the Stonefly Nymph drops way off, and the live nymph becomes the most productive bait. It's virtually impossible to take a trout on an artificial because they are finding food by its smell.

Live nymphs, and later, the adult flies that swarm over the bankbrush, continue to outfish imitations until the flood passes its peak, and the river begins to clear and fall. Then, trout start taking artificials again. The water is clear enough for them to see their food, so the way it smells isn't important.

The stonefly hatch is exceptional, though, and in ways other than its proportions. Most insects aren't active during high or even medium water levels. A large volume of water carries a burden of sediment with it—leaves, sand, and twigs—and it moves a lot of rocks around. Aquatic insects are fragile creatures, and they can't take the pounding and pelting a swollen stream drives before it, so they stay undercover until the stream returns to normal. As a rule, when streams run milky, you're wisest to use a lure.

When water is milky, it is either on the rise or fall in response to runoff or rain. There will be very little aquatic insect activity, and land-based foods are either just entering the stream environment or they've already washed through. Trout then zero in on the most abundant meal around . . . baitfish, and lures amount to the most able imitation of this class of food.

Low, clear, conditions are a signal that flies are probably the most logical offering. You can catch trout on bait or lures then, but never so regularly as with a fly. Somewhere around 90 percent of a trout's diet is made up of insects, and that tells you something about where the real power lies.

In some ways, you can align baitfishing, lure fishing and flyfishing with the same time of the year, too; bait in the early spring, then lures, then flies. But it's wiser to judge the condition of the water on the spot. A heavy rain can occur at any time during trout season, and fish respond to their environment, not the calendar. One of the best days I ever had baitfishing was in August, after a three-day rain. I could not believe the appetite those trout had for a worm, or the numbers of them that were crammed into one hole at the foot of a broken bar. The ironic thing was that after I'd caught so many fish that I grew bored, I stopped by a cafe for a cup of coffee. It was standing-room-only, crowded with fishermen who were lamenting that the fishing would be poor for two to three days until the water cleared.

There is one more judgment to make while we're standing here: that of the velocity of the stream. It doesn't really tell you anything about feeding patterns, but rather it puts functional limits on the tackle you use.

Slow water—lakes, placid currents that barely eddy along, and streams that move along up to three miles per hour—is the ideal condition for a fly rod, and for spinning bait or lures. Moderate to swift currents, three to six miles per hour, are best suited to spinning with bait or lures. Velocities in excess of six miles an hour are fishable with spinning lures alone, and the outer limits of streamflow are simply unworkable.

The reasoning behind these limits has its roots in the consequences of line drag, basically the current's effect on your cast and retrieve. Fly line, because of its diameter, endures the greatest purchase of the current. It becomes difficult, if not impossible, to manage accurately in swift water. It is at the mercy of current vectors rather than your control. This faster water also makes mending, keeping a taut line, and casting difficult when you are working upstream . . . a presentation that produces about 85 percent of the action on a fly. Sinking lines aren't much of a help under these conditions either. When you work them upriver, they give rise to the same problems presented by floating lines. Fished downriver, even high-density lines will elevate as flow velocities increase. I cannot overemphasize the significance of these limits. In fact, I would say the most common mistake flyfishermen make is to attempt to fish three to six miles per hour currents with fly tackle. They take a few trout, which encourages them to hang in there, but they would do so much better if they'd match their tackle to conditions. Always remember, once you determine the most logical tackle, the final ingredient is to find the right water to cast over.

So what has our quick appraisal of Back Brook told us? In a way, too many things. The conditions you have found don't make for an easy decision. It is 10:30 A.M., and the water feels cold but not numbing. Temperatures are probably in the 50-degree range. In waist-deep water, you can see bottom, but not perfect detail; I couldn't call the stream milky, but it isn't exactly clear, either.

The current where you are standing rates within the fly rod limits, but there is whitewater in the riffle below the bridge, and what looks like even swifter, deeper water upstream.

I know. The fish we saw rising has quit us, too.

I would lay sixty-to-forty odds that spinning with a lure is the most likely way to fetch a fat trout. But I'd reached for the fly rod anyway. There's a chance we might be able to persuade them to take a dry, and so long as there is a chance, that's the place I would choose to begin.

Good, then! I hoped you'd agree. Go ahead, go back to the wagon and rig up the fly rod. Rules are made to be broken, anyway.

5 / *Watercraft*

I noticed a few casting problems back at the bridge. Dropping your back cast, mainly. It's a common problem. When we get to some fly water, I'll work with you on that. You probably put that fish down by getting too close to him.

It's just as well that he didn't strike, though. That would have tempted us to stay there, and it's an infallible rule that the distance you put between you and your car will be directly proportional to the quality of the troutfishing you'll find. It's a matter of human rather than trout nature, however. People expect a trout to come easy, so they fish near roads. I know we'll do better by going upstream.

How far? Oh, somewhere between a half-mile and a mile. That's the distance that seems to separate the lazy and the lucky. It will also give us a chance to look the stream over, to get the feel of it. That's the next step. Recognizing a river's movement, and then being able to move with it, to fit in. If you are going to catch a trout, you have to be submissive, not assertive. You have to first give in to the natural schemes that are working around you . . . maybe join them is a better description. But it's the most reliable way to trick a trout.

Do you feel the river's personality beginning to emerge? It's an odd one, I've got to admit. I've never seen anything quite like it, and I've been up to my waist in just about every kind of trout stream you could imagine.

As a rule, each stream fits into a pattern, just like the fish in it, and the pattern is established by the pitch of the bed. The greater the pitch, the faster the water flows. That's why you hear terms like "a classic trout stream," and a "flat water stream." A stream with very little pitch to the bed will have velocities of three miles per hour or less, so you can fish it effectively with any tackle you choose.

As pitches increase, a stream's nature changes. It winds less, there is more swift, white water, and the choices narrow down. It's not purely a matter of one stream being a fly stream exclusively and another a lure stream. Even in the wildest rivers, you can find some fly water, but proportionately, the greater the pitch of the bed, the fewer opportunities there will be to work a fly, then a worm, and finally a lure. To that extent, certain streams and rivers lend themselves best to one technique or another.

Funny thing. Do you see how the volume of water in Back Brook is much greater here than back at the car? It picked up as soon as we got out of that tunnel of overstory and into the open pastures. That was a shock in more ways than volume of water alone. It was so dark and cool and mossy inside that tunnel that even the light was green. The thick leaves made for a great, green filter and the light was so subdued that stepping into the sunlight was like an explosion. Now this . . . strange indeed.

You would think that the river would run up the valley, but there's barely a trickle coming down from there. All the water comes from this canyon. I've seen one other stream like this. It

got trapped in a granite shortcut a million years ago, and cut down into the hard rock, carving nearly vertical walls. In principle, it should have taken another, softer route, but it didn't and geologists don't know why. Then, when it reached the valley where it should have been in the first place, it dropped into a hole called a sink, and disappeared. They poured dye down the sink, chemicals that could be traced . . . they still couldn't find where the river went.

And look at Back Brook now, boiling pools, wild, white water. . . . Brutish rapids. It is very tough fishing in that stuff. Strictly spinning water, but it can hold some ponderous trout. Ever float down through rapids like that in a raft? If you want to talk about exciting troutfishing, it's the ultimate. Your life is on the line as well as the fish you catch.

This is quite a climb. We must have gained 200 feet since we left the valley floor, and it looks even steeper ahead. It's said that the wise man scales a mountain a step at a time and a fool climbs to the top. It's a good attitude to culture. Besides, have you stopped and looked around? That's the same mountain we saw from where we left the car. It looks even prettier from up here. And there are falls up ahead. They're not just a pretty sight, they're a strong suggestion we're heading into a hanging valley, and that there will be gentler water above us. You'll find that streams descend at a fixed rate. If it is the nature of a stream to descend at 40 feet to the mile, and you see that it drops 30 feet in a quarter-mile, the other three-quarters of a mile will probably drop only 10 feet, and that would make for a slow, snaky river. Let's hope I'm right; we haven't run across really ideal flyfishing water below here.

Company! There, in the pool by the side of the falls. A bait-fisherman, by the way he's holding his rod. That's patient sport, that kind of baitfishing; just put a worm on a hook and wait, and a waterfall makes for a good companion. The sound and the sight of it washes your ears and eyes clean, and while you're waiting, you have time to think. It's the most relaxing way of all to catch a trout; not the most likely I've found, but still-fishing by a quiet pool is so easy on the mind that a nibbling fish is practically an intrusion.

My legs tell me that this path is leveling out, and the canyon walls aren't so steep or high now that we've gotten above the falls. I'd say my guess was right, but that's not accurate either. It wasn't really guesswork; understanding how water runs has a lot to do with catching a trout.

I know ... it always runs downstream, but don't bet on that either. I'll put up a 10-dollar-bill that says Back Brook has water that flows upstream; but before you take me up on it, let me warn you that I will win. All streams do.

In fact, if troutfishing has a bottom line, that's it ... water-craft. Understanding how water works, and how trout react to its workings. Being able to read water with accuracy, precision, and solid conviction; to know by the look of the stream that if a trout is around, he will be finning behind that rock, in that midstream surge, or at the foot of those falls we just passed. The kind and quality of your tackle, the perfection of your technique, even the medium that dresses your hook are all subordinate to that skill.

You must begin with the realization that trout always gravitate to the slowest zones in a stream. These are places where they can lie and wait, finning in the gentle current, then rocket out to snare food that swifter waters carry by. If there were no such zones, there would be no fish. Although they're associated with fast, frothy water, no trout could last long in a station where he is fighting more than a two to three mile per hour current. The economics of energy dictate this. So much fat, and then tissue, would be burned up holding in fast water that the intake of food could not replace the bulk lost.

Slow zones most commonly occur right next to the bottom, even in the wildest, whitest rapids. The explanation for this lies in a natural phenomenon called laminar flow.

Water moves downslope in response to gravity, but it does not move uniformly. Even in a square, concrete channel, straight as a superhighway, friction with the channel bed would produce a succession of shear lines that gradually lose velocity as they approach the bottom.

To explain the principle of laminar flow in another way, imagine sheets of glass separated by ball bearings. Assuming resistance to be constant, moving the top layer of glass would have an effect on underlying layers, but the effect would be diminished by 50 percent with each succeeding layer.

If each layer of glass were 6-inches thick, and the top layer were moved at a speed of six miles an hour, the layer of glass at the 3-foot level would be moving at a half mile per hour. Given the latitude of poetic license, this is precisely the condition as it exists with moving water.

But laminar flow has other implications, too. Given our straight, square channel, resistance would also occur against the side of the flume, creating a kind of three-dimensional flow effect, with water achieving maximum velocities in the very

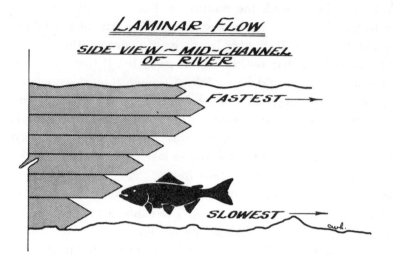

center of the stream. This is precisely the case as it exists with a natural watercourse, but slow zones are also created, enhanced, and defined by things like river bands, boulders, channels, blow-downs, log jams, and the like.

Identifying slow zones is only half of reading water, though. You should also look for some sort of current neck or funnel that has the effect of concentrating whatever food the river might be sweeping along. When slow zones and current necks occur side-by-side, the place is a likely station for a trout.

The easiest way to winnow out these stations is to look first for deep water. Trout are very reluctant to feed in shallows because there they are an easy mark for predators. You'll find it more than rare to catch a trout that you can see, especially in a stream. I have fished to trout I could see in a lake, and occasionally caught one, but even there it is a dubious proposition.

If deep water abuts a shear line, it is a good bet for a cast. Shear lines divide slow and fast water. They are never arrow straight or marked as plainly as a racing stripe, but still they are relatively easy to pick out. More often than not, they are signaled by submerged objects in the stream, or current responses to bed obstructions, known collectively as hydraulics.

Tell you what. Let's leave the path for a few moments and wade up the stream bank. I can probably pick out all the important hydraulics in a hundred yards. I can see several just below us on that flat water.

First look upstream and then down. Do you see the swift water funneling into the widening in the stream bed, and the way the bottom shoals and aprons out below us? You could look at this as a kind of stream unit, a predictable pattern that repeats itself again and again. The only variable will be velocity, which will define the most practical tackle to use.

The temptation is to call this place a pool, but I think there should be a more exacting vocabulary. So for now, let's just recognize it as a place where the stream slows, deepens, then widens and flows over shallows.

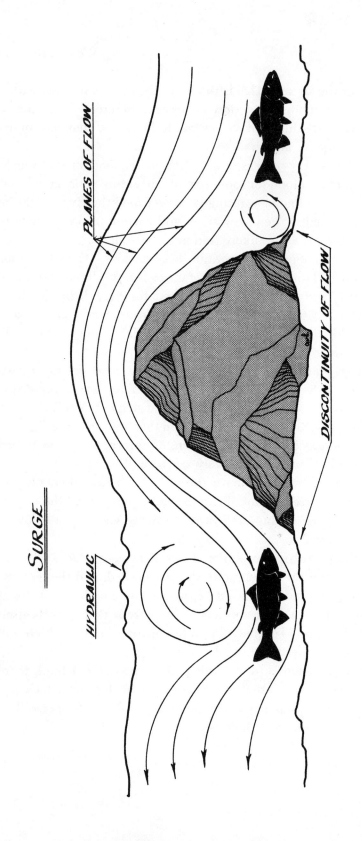

SURGE

HYDRAULIC

PLANES OF FLOW

DISCONTINUITY OF FLOW

Let's look at those shallows first. See how clear they are? Pretty too, with gold and gray trapezoidal rocks laid down along the bottom. But not a very good place to fish, at least right now. If there were a major hatch going on, trout would move out there to feed, and they might be there when the light is so low and slanting that you couldn't see bottom, but I would bet you couldn't coax a hit right now, and if trout were feeding there that they would be relatively small. It's a popular place to fish, especially with a fly, because it's easy. But there are no current necks to concentrate food, and there's no place for a large fish to hide.

Now follow the bed upstream, just to the point where the bottom becomes unclear and the water appears milky. Line that place up with the big beech tree across the current. Halfway between you and it, troubled water keeps burping up, as if it were a huge fish rolling to the surface. That hydraulic is called a surge.

A surge is the current's response to an underwater object; a sunken log, boulder, or a waving thatch of weed. As it moves over and around the obstruction, a discontinuity of flow forms just below it, a little like the low pressure above an airplane's wing. It's that discontinuity of flow that is winking on and off.

Surges are a good bet for a decent fish. There is virtually no current behind them, and when they occur in a deep-current lane, they serve as a food neck.

Now, using that same beech tree as a reference point, follow the opposite shore upstream to those upturned roots. See how that log juts into the water? That's called a sweeper.

Sweepers are blowdowns or floatdowns that reach into the water from the shore. By virtue of their angle of entry, part of the log is above water and part of it is below. They create a condition similar to a surge, where trout can get down out of the current. I've found them even more promising than a surge, though, because they are anchored to the bank. Bank stations are usually more attractive to trout than midstream hides because the land provides an additional food supply to whatever is flow-

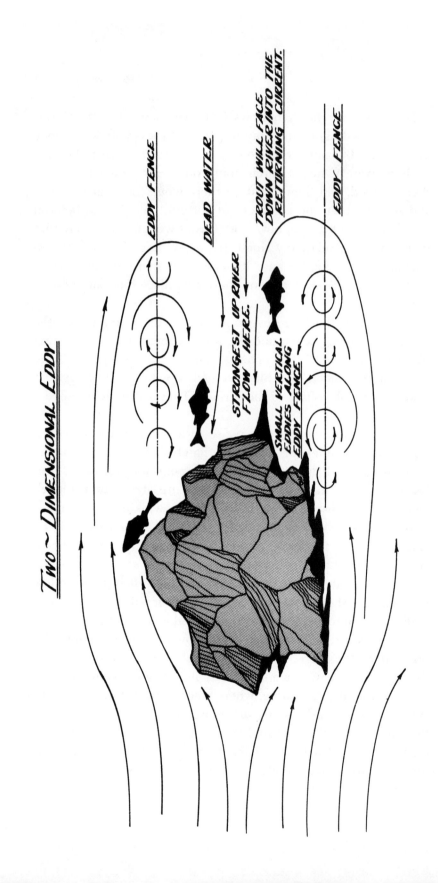

Two~Dimensional Eddy

EDDY FENCE

DEAD WATER

TROUT WILL FACE DOWN RIVER INTO THE RETURNING CURRENT.

STRONGEST UP RIVER FLOW HERE.

SMALL VERTICAL EDDIES ALONG EDDY FENCE

EDDY FENCE

ing along with the stream. Something else about sweepers is that they don't normally occur in swift currents. Heavy water washes them someplace else. So they're always a good place to fish a fly.

Now come out from that sweeper into midcurrent. See that layer-cake of a boulder? It is forming what is called a two-dimensional eddy.

Two-dimensional eddies occur as water flows around both sides of an emerged obstruction. The primary or downstream current forms two shear lines of elevated water, a little like the bow waves created by a boat. This, in turn, causes a hole to form between the lines and behind the obstruction, creating a kind of vacuum effect that actually sucks water upriver. The point of meeting of those two opposing currents is called the "eddy fence."

Two-dimensional eddies are highly probable stations for trout. The quiet zone behind the boulder offers access to both shear lines, and the cleaving of the current by the boulder tends to concentrate the field of food that rushes by the eddy fence. But two-dimensional eddies are deceptive in one way. Trout stationed behind the boulder will be looking downstream, not up. Trout always fin into the current, and this is one case where the current in the station is opposite the pitch of the river bed.

Now follow the eddy fence to the point where it disappears. The tail of a two-dimensional eddy is another likely spot for a fish. It is the place where conflicting currents reach accord, very nearly dead water, and trout take to it like horses to apples.

Another abiding principle to grasp is that size has little to do with hydraulics. Water responds to a pebble in the same way it does to a boulder. If you dropped a stone in a tiny trickle, and its top were above water, it would create a two-dimensional eddy with the same characteristics as the one you're looking at now, just smaller. The same is true of velocities. Two-dimensional eddies occur in raging water. Like the current, they are more violent, with higher elevation along the eddy fence and a swifter reflex current, but they take the same form nonetheless, and they will hold fish. It may be impossible to get to them when they are

Riverbend & Pool

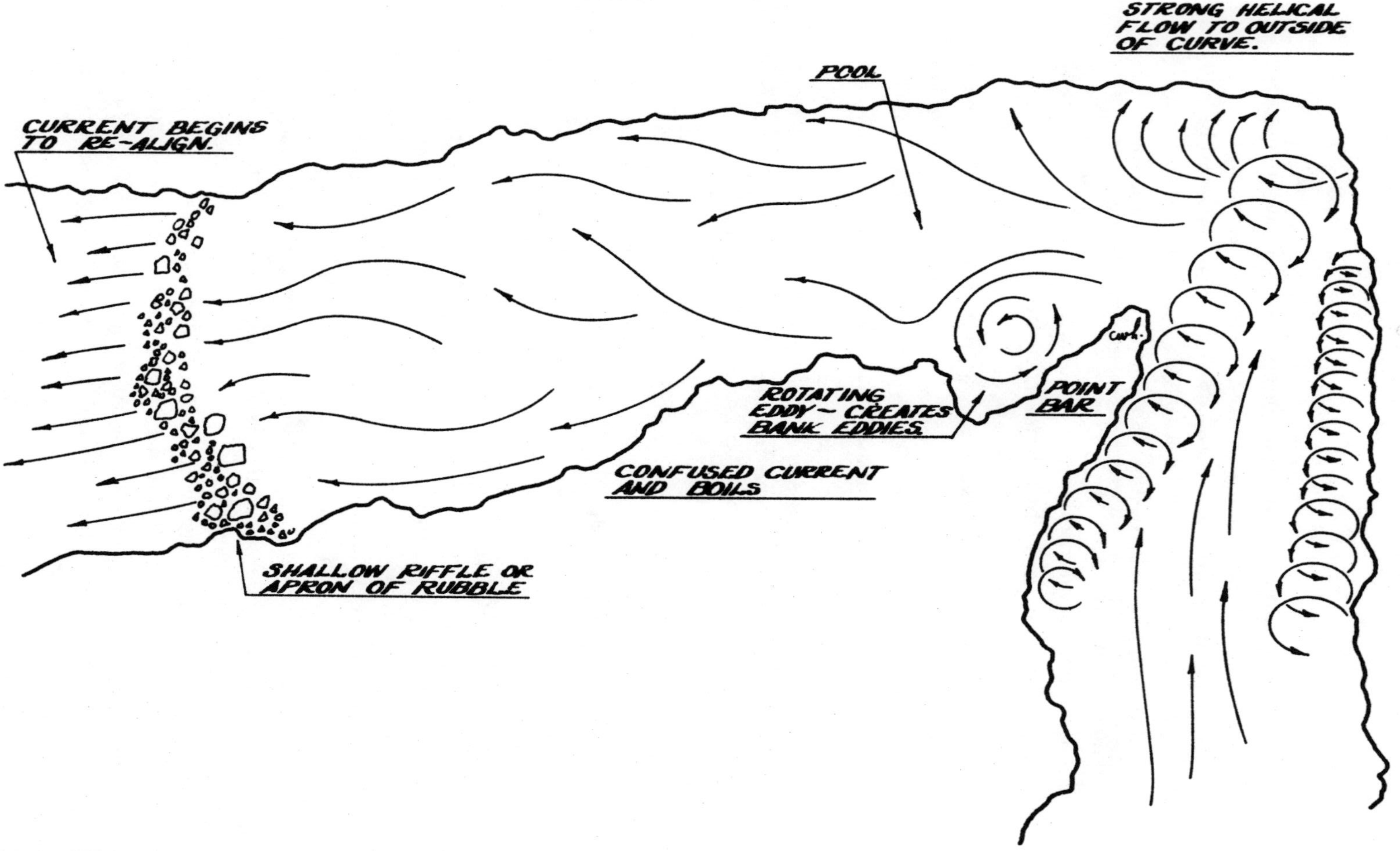

STRONG HELICAL FLOW TO OUTSIDE OF CURVE.

POINT BAR

POOL

ROTATING CREATES EDDY— BANK EDDIES

CONFUSED CURRENT AND BOILS

SHALLOW RIFFLE OR APRON OF RUBBLE

CURRENT BEGINS TO RE-ALIGN.

really wild, though. That's why recognizing the functional limitations to tackle is so important.

The rest of the flat water that lies between us, the eddy, and the sweeper. There could be a fish or two finning right next to the bottom, but unless I saw fish rising, I would not spend too much time working it over. I see no reason for a trout to be there. Do not fish at random. At the very least, you should fish to a probability.

Now let's move up toward the head of this widening, and see if it should be called a pool or not. The term is one of the most overworked in trout fishing, and thus it is imprecise. I've heard it used to identify every form of stream morphology from two-dimensional eddies to broken bars.

I call a pool, a deep, very slow spot in a river, where lines of flow become confused, and where you can't see bottom. Pools occur at a widening in the stream bed, downriver of a bend or a riffle.

. . . Yes, I would call this a pool. See how the rapids rush into that deep hole? Watch the surface; it swirls and boils and rolls, but it has no real direction until it gets downriver. A mixmaster, and very poor fishing.

Big pools like this are tough to fish because the only stations are down deep, close to the bottom. The confusion of currents also creates no necking of the food supply. Remember that in order for a trout to take a bait, he has to see it first, and even with a heavy spinning lure, it would be difficult to get it down in front of the fish. Pools are worm holes, and not very good ones at that, except when they occur in small streams. There are different forces at work there . . . a lot of food and limited stations, so trout will locate in pools then. The test is easy. If you can see some sign of bottom, fish a pool. If you can't, pass it up.

I see you are puzzled, and I'm not surprised. You've always heard that pools are one of the most likely places for trout to be. Well, don't forget how the average trout fishmerman kicks the term around, that's half your misunderstanding. The other half is

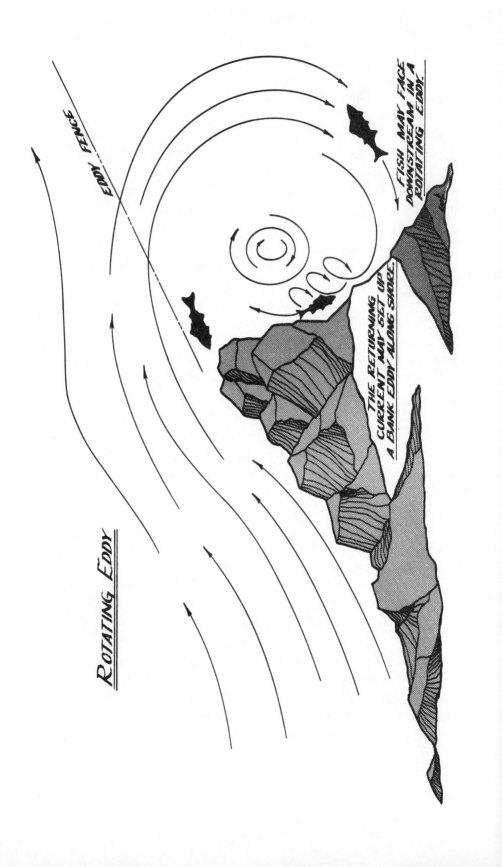

ROTATING EDDY

EDDY FENCE

FISH MAY FACE DOWNSTREAM IN A ROTATING EDDY.

THE RETURNING CURRENT MAY SET UP A BANK EDDY ALONG SHORE.

that it's true, there are times when the bottom of big pools are paved with trout. But I've found these to be the same times when they are utterly off feed for one reason or another; sullen, shy, and reluctant to take any kind of bait. If you can't get a rise anywhere else, no matter how skillfully or hard you try, you might then be able to take a trout from a deep pool using a big, heavy lure or drowning a worm. But I would not call the prospects red-hot.

You may also be confusing the term "pools" with "runs." To explain the difference between the two, we'll have to look at a third term, "thalweg." The thalweg of a stream is roughly synonymous with "main stream channel," the deepest part of a live stream bed at any given point. Thalwegs characteristically wander from side to side in a riverbed, and have a relatively constant depth. When the thalwegs straighten, elongate, and deepen, a run is formed. Unlike pools, there is no confusion of currents in a run; lines of flow remain parallel. If conditions are clear, you will also be able to see the bottom in a run. As in pools, however, downriver movement in a run will be slow in comparison to the stream average. The hydraulics in runs are excellent for trout, one of the most fishable of all stream conditions, perfectly suited to a fly.

In a way, the same dynamics of water created pools and runs, but pools are great, scooped-out pockets. Runs are more gentle. Because of their brotherhood, however, the same hydraulics commonly occur at the head of each.

Look carefully where we are standing. The water is shallow on this side, and deep on the other side. It is rushing into this pool on about a 45-degree angle, and it appears that we are standing on a peninsula of deposited stream rock. Notice the water just below the peninsula. See how it is moving in a circle? That's called a rotating eddy.

Rotating eddies are set to whirling when a current comes into conflict with an obstruction anchored to the bank. The result of this conflict is a reflex flow of water that whirls out and away from the primary current, then circles around to join it once again. On a grand scale, a whirlpool is one example of a rotating eddy.

Small rotating eddies may be set in motion by trees at the water's edge, bank irregularities, or shore rock. Large rotating eddies usually occur on a sharp riverbend, and they are often created by a sedimentary deposit called a point bar. That's what this peninsula is. Whatever the cause of a rotating eddy, its effect is to carve out a deep hole immediately below the obstruction, the more prominent the obstruction, the larger the hole.

Rotating eddies have an eddy fence. It stretches from the tip of the obstruction causing it to the place where the reflex and mainstream currents part. No matter what the size of the rotating eddy, trout will be stationed along the eddy fence. It is almost a sure thing that there will be a fish waiting just inside the apex of the angle formed by the returning reflex current meeting the primary stream current. This station will be located only a few feet from the tip of the obstruction that is causing the eddy.

In the largest rotating eddies, the reflex current is often stiff enough to set up bank eddies along the shore, and fish will be stationed there. Rotating eddies are also set in motion on either side of a waterfall. That's where that fellow was fishing below here. He had his rod poked right into the apex of a rotating eddy. It's great water for a worm, lure, or fly.

Rotating eddies have one thing in common with two-dimensional eddies; parts of them are moving upriver, so you have to fish them with your wits about you. Remember that a trout that can see you will never bite, and if you cast to a fish that is oriented with his head toward you, the chances are high that he will see you.

Now look across-stream. See how the current is slamming into that tall bank? It hits, curls over, and becomes realigned to the new direction the bed is taking. Just downstream of that curl is a bank eddy.

Bank eddies occur in response to bank friction compounded by a secondary flow. They are signaled when deep water passes by a steep bank, and they are revealed by an obscure eddy fence paralleling the shoreline, inside of which surface currents tumble and boil.

Bank eddies will occur along a straight stretch of shoreline. They are more commonly found on the outside of a sharp bend, like the one where a cut bank turns the direction of the water.

Bank eddies are extremely fertile conditions for trout, because food is concentrated by the current along the eddy fence due to another property of moving water called helical flow. This is a corkscrewing, spiraling current secondary to laminar flow, that

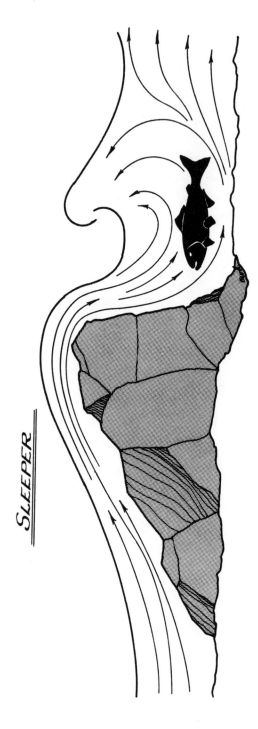

SLEEPER

moves slowly out from shore into the swiftest part of the river. Facing downstream, helical flow circles clockwise on your left, counterclockwise on your right.

When streamflow bumps into a bend, helical flow becomes dominant, rolling the river up, out, and over, converting the energy of forward motion into a spiral. This has the effect of a ferris wheel, turning slowly in front of the eddy fence, presenting virtually all the food carried by the river to that station. Bank eddies also have the extra appeal provided by the introduction of land-oriented foods. You will find them to be one of the most reliable stations in a stream.

Every hydraulic below us, from this point bar to the aproning riffle where we first joined the river, is a potential station for trout. But there is very little fishable water above us. Rapids make for poor fishing, so let's just get above them. No use in spending a lot of time in water that looks like that.

There's one hydraulic of interest in this swifter water, though—a sleeper. Sleepers are stream obstructions, usually boulders very close to the surface. Water passes up and over the top of a sleeper, then cleaves into a discontinuity of flow behind it, creating a stationary wave that falls back on itself. If you'll recall the babbling brooks you've known, it's the sleepers that do all the babbling.

Trout station themselves behind sleepers, but they can be hard to fish. Small sleepers with waves that barely lap and break make for perfect flyfishing conditions. More violent sleepers that crash and roar can be fished only with spinning gear. The plane of flow that cleaves the water behind a big sleeper usually amounts to an· impossible barrier for a fly line. Because of its thick diameter, a fly line won't cut through to where the fish are. Size up any sleeper with a careful eye, however. The vast majority of sleepers will occur in shallow water where they'll harbor only small trout, and that's what I'd judge to be in this water. It's all shallow sleepers and two-dimensional eddies, pretty to see and hear, but not the best fishing.

One moment . . . ever see a water ouzel? There's one right there, that drab, gray little bird standing on top of the rock right across from us. Watch him. He'll disappear in a few seconds.

See that? The crazy things can actually walk underwater. They get on top of a sleeper and catch the current that cleaves the water, and it carries them to the bottom. Then they use it to hold them there while they pick around for nymphs.

Now he's up again, bouncing around like a sandpiper.

They winter on Quicksilver Creek, and that's an odd thing about them, too. I've never heard them sing in the summer, but when it is cold enough to break axeblades, and Quicksilver is etched with hoarfrost, they sing the sweetest, clearest song I have ever heard. It's a joy to hear them when it's 20 below . . . like a prayer for spring.

Do you recognize that spot just ahead where the rapids begin? Anything familiar about it?

No, I don't mean to suggest that you've been here before, just that there is another principle to be recognized, another pattern. This is really where we began, at the riffle below a pool, and we are here again. That is basically the way a river is put together; the stream unit I mentioned earlier. Riffle, rapids, flat water, riffle, and within that major geography, the individual hydraulics, and within the hydraulics, the trout. It is the same with all rivers and streams and brooks, just on different scales of size and velocity.

Remember the one-to-seven ratio? What's the distance between pools? It comes pretty close, doesn't it? It is a kind of cycle, or maybe a circle is a better description.

Another interesting cycle you find involves the way in which trout respond to the fertility of each stream environment, and the dictates of their species. In very fertile streams like Quicksilver Creek and the Gunflint, trout station themselves in much faster water than what has proven to be the norm. They will strike way outside of an eddy fence, and even move right up into a riffle when there is a lot of food washing down. I also find trout

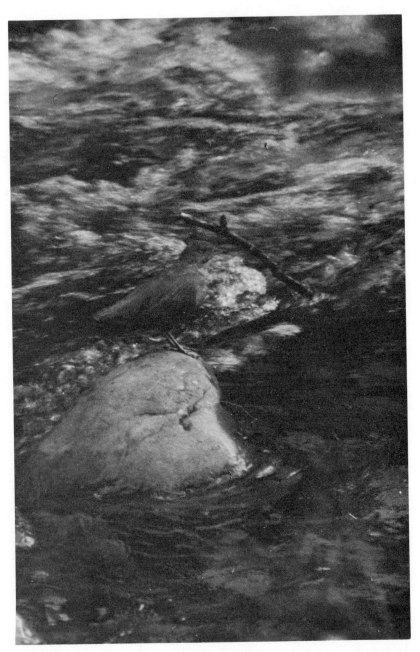

A water ouzel

of fair size and numbers in the bubble-shot water behind sleepers in rapids in these streams. This uncommon behavior probably comes from the amount of food available. There is so much of it that the fish can afford to expend the energy it takes to fight a swift current. And it has a delightful side-effect, bringing out the best in a trout. Quicksilver brookies jump like rainbows, and the rainbows and browns in the Gunflint tear up tackle and turn out to be 12 inches long. They are magnificent in conformation too, with bullet-like bodies, sleek and strong and trim. There are surely parallels that could be drawn with principles of physical conditioning. When there is a perfect balance between diet and exercise, physique and stamina are its compliment.

Another pattern that clusters around current velocities is segregation by species. The gentlest reflex currents are favored by brook trout. Browns favor slightly faster water, and rainbows gravitate toward the fastest water. In a large, rotating eddy, brookies would congregate in the slack water near the hub of rotation, or inside the quiet bank eddies along shore. Browns would most probably be found at the confluence of the primary and reflex current, and rainbows would station themselves right along the eddy fence. This sorting is interesting in that it is also a reflection of stamina. In terms of pound-for-pound clout, I would rate a rainbow the most energetic fish on the end of a line and a brookie the least. When you get good at streamcraft, you can make an educated guess at the species of trout on the end of your line on the basis of where the strike occurred, and be right about 75 percent of the time.

There is one time, however, when reading water is an unnecessary exercise: when trout are actively rising. As a matter of fact, it could be a counterproductive. The insect activity that triggers a surface feed is pretty much a random process with flies and rises blooming everywhere, so zero in on a dimpling fish and work to him rather than the river. This is one of the great pleasures of a substantial rise; neither special skills nor guesswork are involved in finding a fish.

When trout are not on the rise, however, you have to fish to stations, and there is one more to see, perhaps the best spot of all for a trout. Look carefully at the riffle that forms at the foot of this next pool. . . . Riffles result when a stream passes over a shallow cobble- or pebble-sized bed. Small sleepers and two-dimensional eddies form a kind of mini-rapid. It is too shallow for stations for large fish, but riffles are a stream's food factory. Fry and insects thrive in the sunlit, oxygen-charged, predator-free atmosphere of a riffle in greater numbers than in any other part of the stream. Should a station occur just below a riffle, it is the most likely spot of all to harbor a trout.

The forces that create a riffle, however, are not complimentary to most of the hydraulics we looked at. Most riffles race into rapids by a gradual deepening of the bed. The exception is the broken riffle or broken bar, a riffle with the equivalent of a run below it.

If there is anything difficult about finding this glory hole—this riffle with a run below it—it is identifying its existence. There are no stark swirls or granite monuments to mark its place, only subtle clues.

Look first at the character of the riffles. If it is uniform in depth, with roughly an equal volume of water passing over the shallows from bank to bank, it is a strong indication that the water immediately below will have no dramatic change in its bed; that bottom contours will gradually deepen, or narrow, or both, setting up no large quiet zones where trout can bank up.

If, however, the riffle aprons out to shoal in places and channel in others, high water probably has carved out holes below. Look especially for currents that slow over brightly-colored water, and then flow laterally. Watch the lateral movement until it realigns itself, and begins to head downriver once again. These places where the water is gathering itself up are channels in the riffle.

Follow the flow of water down the channel. In strong sunlight, the color of the stream will dim and darken over the top of the channel, and the sides of the channel—the shallow riffle area— will remain bright.

Somewhere downstream, the whole riffle-and-channel complex

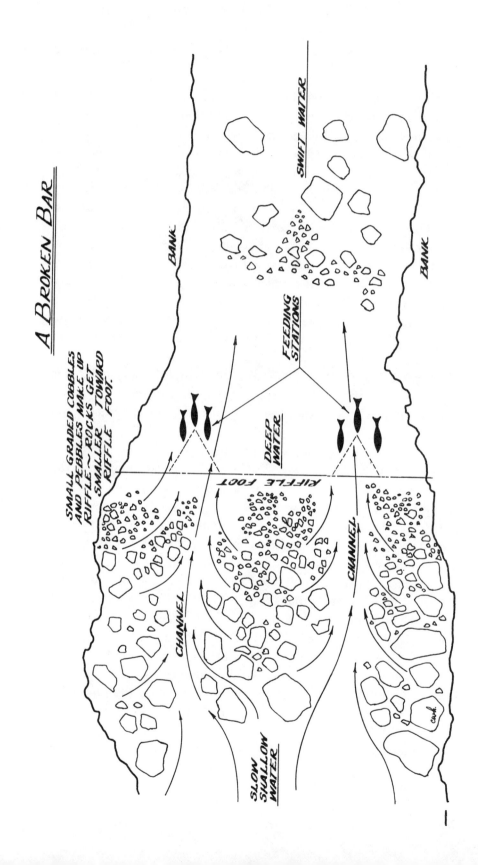

A Broken Bar

BANK

SWIFT WATER

SMALL GRADED COBBLES AND PEBBLES MAKE UP RIFFLE~ROCKS GET SMALLER TOWARD RIFFLE FOOT.

FEEDING STATIONS

DEEP WATER

RIFFLE FOOT

CHANNEL

CHANNEL

SLOW SHALLOW WATER

BANK

should end abruptly. It may be signaled by the same kind of breaking wave that results from a sleeper, but even if the wave isn't there, you should be able to identify the spot by water color as the shallow riffle suddenly drops off into a hole. The center of feeding activity will occur below the middle of the channel, and at the apex of an imaginary perfect triangle, formed by taking the distance from shallow riffle to shallow riffle, across the channel, as its base.

You can also identify a broken riffle by the appearance of the stream surface. This is an even more reliable yardstick than color, since it works with dirty water. Watch for lateral movement of water over a riffle, movement that suddenly changes direction and heads downstream. Then follow it with your eye. The currents over the channel will be swift and the water of a rough texture. The texture will gradually smooth out, then rear up into small, irregular waves ... troubled water. This results from the planes of flow established by the channel conflicting with the drag set up by the still water of a deep hole. These irregular waves will be stationary, like the wave behind a sleeper, yet if you trace the path of a bubble or a twig, it will pass up and over them. Trout will be stationed underneath these irregular waves, just beneath the plane of rapid channel current.

Get to know the look of broken bars well. When they occur, they are often virgin water, even in streams that receive heavy fishing pressure, because most fishermen don't know they're there. They also represent the key to fishing large, young rivers that appear to be one big riffle from beginning to end. If you study the surface carefully, you'll find broken bars everywhere.

That's the main difference, incidentally, between fishing in the West and fishing in the East. Ultimately, it is a matter of hydraulics. In terms of geology, the West is much younger than the East. Wind, ice, water, and time have not worked so long on the valleys and the mountains, so the riverbeds are steep. I would say twice as steep, on the average, as in the East. A graceful Eastern stream drops at around 20 feet to the mile. In the wild West, streams often drop 40 feet to the mile.

As a result, western streams are powerful and dramatic. Sleepers, two-dimensional eddies, rapids, point bars, rotating eddies, bottomless pools, and broken bars predominate. There are quieter waters, but they are usually in smallish streams that have been tamed by a flat valley floor. Swift waters also create a kind of impersonality about western streams. Visually, at least, they are barren-banked and monotonous. The trout are surely there to break the monotony, in greater numbers and of greater size than in the East, but they tend to be channel-oriented, gravitating toward the middle of watercourses where they are difficult to reach and hard to read. Troutfishing in the West is technically difficult and physically demanding; and especially flyfishing, because there isn't a great deal of three mile per hour water.

The East is old geographically. Its streams have had an opportunity to settle down in comfortable niches. There are few deep pools and fewer violent rapids. What rapids exist consist of sleepers and two-dimensional eddies in short sequences that stair-step from run to run at fishable velocities. Banks are stable, with a lot of sweepers, and vegetation towers above them lush, green and rich-appearing. The trout seem to recognize this, too. They are far more bank-oriented than those in the West. Eastern streams are also more intimate and more easily interpreted and fished. If I could order Paradise, I would immediately transfer the trout of the West to the streams of the East and never roam again.

No, that's not true. I enjoy the roaming nearly as much as the fishing. Poking around, making new discoveries, just like today. So let's push on just a little further. This canyon seems to be opening up even more, which is another suggestion of gentle water ahead. Maybe even a lake. That could be fun, too.

Read a lake? Sure, you can interpret it with an eye to where the trout will likely be, and it's even easier than a river, because trout don't have to find that delicate blend of quiet zones and feeding lanes. A lake amounts to one big quiet zone, so food is the only thing you'll have to find, and the first place to look for it is in any kind of current.

Wherever you find a current in a lake, you will find trout. Generally, the closer you get to the current source, the more trout will be concentrated there.

Inlet streams are the most popular spot of all. Not only do they wash food in, they also wash in sediment, which creates alluvium; shoals and mudbanks which function as plant farms and food factories. Look for banks where slow currents pass over shoals, and then pitch off to lake depths, and you will find cruising fish. It's the same principle as a broken bar.

If a lake has an inlet and an outlet, that lake will have a current lane, a "stream" of moving water within dead lake water, with limits nearly as constant and definable as the banks of a stream. These current lanes are sometimes hard to perceive in lakes, because they might be moving at a quarter-mile per hour, but they will exist and trout will concentrate along them.

Current lanes are easiest to identify on quiet days. When there is a light breeeze, watch any windriff that develops on the lake. If the wind direction is with the flow of the current lane, the lane will be calm when the rest of the lake is riffled. If the wind blows against the current's direction, the current lane will riffle before the lake.

If the lake is flat calm, watch for movement of floating objects to indicate moving water. If you are in a boat, and it isn't anchored, you will drift toward the lake outlet when you are over a current lane and remain stationary if you are in dead water. You can make an even more positive judgment by dropping anchor. If you are over a current lane, the slack will leave the anchor line and the boat will head up into the current and hold there.

There are other sources of moving water in lakes, too. Submerged springs are gathering places for trout, but they are difficult to find because they seldom spew out enough water to create a current lane. They are usually discovered by trial and error; you seem to catch more trout in one spot than another, so you fish there. Then some old-timer tells you that you're fishing over "Hidden Springs."

Lake structure is another factor to look at. Currents may be spawned around submerged landforms, such as cliffs and banks, by wind action or thermal inversions. Currents of this kind are usually seasonal, though; a point of land might mark thick concentrations of fish in the spring and fall, and be as barren as the Sahara at other times. The reason for this usually lies either in disturbances created as the lake "turns over," or in the prevailing winds at a particular time of year. Fishing the structure of a lake is a highly individual exercise. As a rule, the most knowledgeable structure fishermen are people who visit a lake often, and come to know its moods by trial and error.

One big clue to their location that trout in lakes provide, that their stream and river counterparts don't, is in the pattern of their surface feeding. Concentrations of rising fish are a pretty reliable indication that the water underneath the dimples functions as a station for these fish at other times, too.

Now there's a sight. Mountaingate. The canyon walls swung open, and there's the valley. Meriwether Lewis and William Clark, you and I, and I name this place Mountaingate. Did you ever read their journals? Truly an incredible journey, and the trout fishing they found in the West makes one weep for the kingdoms we've lost. I get the feeling that they got a little bored with naming places and rivers, though, or perhaps they just ran out of ideas. I keep getting this scenario; Lewis and Clark come upon another river, the seventy-eighth one without a name or a place on the map, and Lewis says, "Go ahead, Clark, you name this one." Clark replies; "But Lew, I did the last one." "Aw c'mon, Clark, I've run out of ideas, and I did the dishes last night." It's one explanation why there is a Clark's Fork and a Lewis River and a Lewis Fork and a Clark Fork and Lewis Creeks and Clark Creeks that won't quit. They probably didn't pack a dictionary.

And that's why Back Brook is the color and the coldness it is. See those hazy-blue mountains way off in the distance? The peaks are white as shark's teeth. It's still being fed by snow runoff. Snowfields yet, and in these mountains! That's the kind of thing you find when you get away from roads.

I'll tell you another thing we've found. The perfect place to drop a dry-fly. The current through these meadows is so slow and the back of the river so smooth that you can see the mountains reflected in it.

No . . . I wouldn't rig the rod yet. Let's just stream watch for a few moments, like that heron is doing by the bend of the river. Beautiful birds, Great Blue Herons. They hunt with such patient grace. . . .

There . . . did you see it? That curling little slap of water in the dark reflection of the other bank? Well, watch; you'll see the ripples ring out. That's something you've got to learn too, to pick out a rise from the zebra patterns of moving water.

Remember what I said about looking at a river with your head as well as your eyes? That's how you see a rise and a station and the places where a fish would never be. It's really what watercraft is all about, and it takes only about 30 seconds next to a stream to see what I've been saying for the last 30 minutes. You just look at the whole stream at once, and you see patterns and irregularities and conflicting currents; the glint of sunlight, and the splash of a rising fish. It's the same as seeing in the dark. The trick is not to concentrate on any one point. Get inside the eye of a hawk and look for a mouse in a field 1,000 feet below, or in the eye of a deer who can see a hunter coming 100 yards away from the back of his head with one eye closed. Then you can forget the thalwegs and rotating eddies and helical flows and look at a stream and say, "there is where the trout will be." And they will be there.

Now, let's see if he will come up again, and if we can get some idea of what he's feeding on.

There, against the shadows. Do you see that whitish bit of fluff caught in the sunlight? Watch it. It's going to touch down right at the head of the bank eddy where the fish is stationed.

Are you following it?

There he is again, just like a firecracker going off. You saw it, didn't you? Mark the spot in the center of the ripples that remain. That's where he's waiting.

6 / *The Mayfly Conspiracy*

A Light Cahill would be my guess; about a #14. Use a 5X tippet; the water isn't crystal clear, but it is as calm as a lake where the trout is rising. And don't forget to use leader sink.

Is your heart beating a little faster? Do you feel the circle drawing in? It happens every time, doesn't it? I don't know how many times I've been part of this moment before, but its effect is never diminished by experience.

And I'll tell you why; to see a rising trout is to become a hunter. Catch a trout any other way and he doesn't exist until he is on the hook, and fishing to probabilities and expectations keeps the distance of anonymity between fisherman and fish. When you know a trout is there and feeding, a line is drawn between the two of you as sure and straight as a gunshot, and the fish has instant dimension, character, and being. To catch him becomes an exclusive contest between the two of you, and that is part of what makes fishing on top what it is: high drama.

That's the second time I've seen you drop the line and watched it slide through the guides to the ground. Relax. It happens to me too, at times like these. It's because you have already connected to the fish, and it's hard to concentrate on other things. It will help if you look at the rod instead of the rise, and double the fly line at the end. Thread it through that way. It's easier to see, and there's more there for your fingers to grab.

Do you know Francis Fortier? He is a concert violinist, and the only one I have ever known who would dare call his Stradivarius a fiddle. But he calls flyfishing playing a violin; the mending hand presses and manipulates strings, the casting hand holds the bow. It's an intriguing comparison.

No . . . don't tie that kind of knot. Clip the snell loop off the leader with your pocket knife, and tie it to the fly line with a nail knot. Another minor detail of major importance. Let me show you.

Every other connecting knot either leaves a tag end of line

hanging on the leader side of the knot, or requires a loop in the fly line. When you have a tag end hanging out, it catches in the snake guides of a fly rod as line is payed out. It's also annoying when you mend line down beyond the knot, and if you fight a fish right down to the leader, which will be necessary when you're using these 9-foot leaders, you'll chance losing him if he gets a second wind, surges away, and the tag hangs up. A loop in the end of the line, whipped like a guide-winding, is another option. It passes through the guides as easily as a nail knot, but I don't like it as well. It makes too big a splash when it lays down.

You know the clinch knot? That's the one to use for the Cahill. It's the universal terminal knot, good for anything you want to tie to the end of monofilament line. But first, you might try clearing the eye of the fly with the point of one of those hooks sticking in the lambswool of my vest. I have a habit of being too generous with head cement when I tie flies, and it clogs the eye shut. If that doesn't make threading the Cahill easier, the next things you might try are eyeglasses.

How many times have you flyfished before? Have you ever had professional instruction? Then before you present the fly, let me see if I can't teach you to handle a little more line. Casting a fly isn't difficult, it's just different from spinning and baitcasting because you are using the weight of the line to reach out rather than the weight of a lure or sinker. That's why fly line is so thick and heavy—so that it has some weight.

You get some funny misunderstandings about it too. Last week I was fishing up north, and I asked a farmer if I could do some fishing in a little meadow stream that ran through his cow pasture.

"What are you going to use?" he asked.

For a second I thought that he was going to tell me that he didn't allow anything but flyfishing, but when I said the stream looked about the right color for worms, he actually seemed relieved.

"Well, at least you got some sense," he said. "Them damn

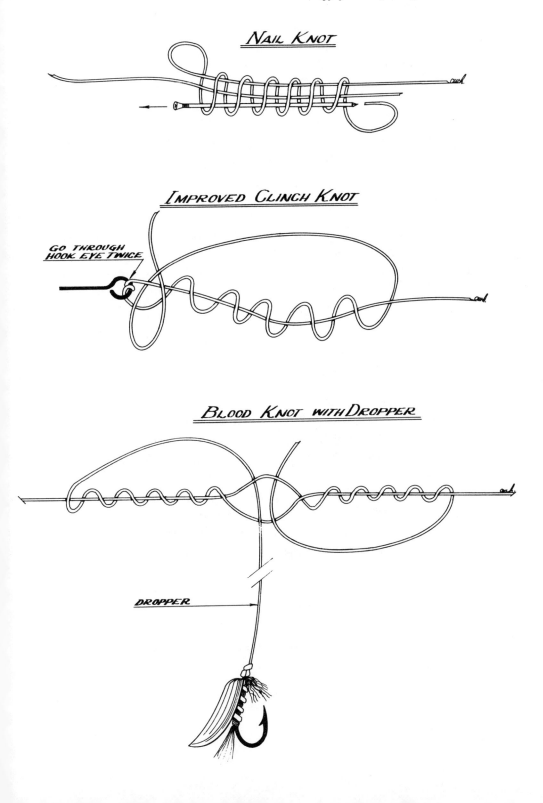

fools from the city come out here with great big rods and use line that's thick enough to rope a cow. Then they put three pound thread on the end of it. Now you figure that one out!"

Nice little insight into how others see us. I'll have to remember to tell Francis.

You do the same thing I do . . . clip the tag end of leader off the knot with your teeth. Scissors are easier in a way, but they're on the knife that's in my pants pocket, deep inside my waders. Wrestling it out of there, opening it, using it, and putting it back is too much effort compared to the quick click of ever-ready incisors.

Now dress the fly with a good dousing in silicone floatant, and cover the last of the leader with sink. Be very careful that the sink doesn't slop over onto the fly. The best way to prevent that is to pin the line over the hole in the top of the bottle with your thumb, turn the bottle upside down, and draw it through to the fly.

Okay, let's try some practice casting before you move up to the fish. If you don't get your backcast straight from the start, you're going to develop bad habits.

When you first strip line from a fresh reel, always stretch it as it comes off, especially the line that is buried deep in the reel arbor. Those curly little sets that the fly line develops when it's been on the reel, even if only overnight, can really foul themselves as you cast. Flycasting requires that you keep quite a few things under control, and a spaghetti tangle at your butt guide doesn't exactly promote smooth coordination.

Let me explain your problem first. You're not getting distance because you're not loading your rod, and you're not loading your rod because you're dropping your backcast. The line is developing a broad "S" behind you, rather than laying out straight. As a result, on the final shooting cast, you're unable to pit the full weight of the line against the recoil of the rod and the power of your arm. You're really propelling only about half of the line's weight, so inertia is not sufficient to carry the full length of line past you and out to your target. It drops down in front of you like a stone, in a slinky compression of coils.

Your problem can be pegged to one of two causes, or perhaps to both. Dropping the rod tip below the One O'clock position on your backcast, and losing your timing. The former puts a deep belly in your line, which is enhanced by bad timing: executing a forward cast before the line has had a chance to straighten out behind you.

Concentrate on stopping your backcast with the tip of your rod between Twelve and One O'clock. It is extremely helpful to watch someone else with the same difficulty, while you coach each other. The One O'clock position is not nearly so far back as your arm and wrist might suggest. You need someone to say, "Stop there," "There," and "There" to get the feel of its location.

To get a handle on timing, commit to memory that the more line you are handling, the longer you will have to pause between forward and backcasts for it to straighten out. When you have 25 feet of line in the air, there is virtually no cause for pause. When you are handling 25 yards, there is about a 2-second pause between the back and forward sweep of the rod.

Here too, it's extremely helpful to have someone standing off to the side, calling the precise moment when the line is laid out straight in back of you. Turning around to look requires an awkward stance that interferes with your cast, and negates much of the body's sensitivity to the feel of a loaded rod.

Recognizing this "loading" by feel rather than rote is really the key to handling maximum lengths of line. There is a point when the energy of the rearward-moving line is perfectly balanced against the power of the rod shaft. It is a moment of stasis, when everything is stopped for a split-second. The line is straight behind and motionless in the air. The rod shaft is poised like a tight spring. At this flickering instant, the rod is fully loaded, and the line can be driven forward at maximum velocities, which translates into maximum ranges.

One trick that will help you learn how to feel loading is lawn practice. Using an old fly line, concentrate only on distance. After reaching your current maximum range, let the line settle to the grass in front of you, and backcast. Let it settle again, making sure it's straight. Peel off some line and forward cast. So long as the line is straight behind you, a strong forward sweep will very nearly load the rod. Lay out as much line as you can handle this way, letting it fall to the ground after each pickup. Concentrate on long, straight casts, on distance without the additional confusion of trying to keep the line in the air. When you are satisfied that you have increased your range on the ground, graduate to a pickup, backcast, and forward cast. Let the cast settle, then pickup, backcast, and forward cast. Feel the rod load on the backcast.

Ultimately, work at false casting. You will not be able to false cast the same amount of line as you had lain before you, but you will be able to keep more line in the air than before, once you know the feel of a loaded rod.

Two other suggestions; use a line one number heavier than is suggested by your rod's manufacturer, and practice casting with a weight-forward taper. Both measures help you feel that moment of loading because your rod will have to work harder. . . . That's a little better, but you are still developing a slack "S" behind you. Concentrate on the One O'clock position, you're coming back too far.

There . . . There . . . There . . . Too far. Did you feel it? How there was less resistance to your forward cast on that last backcast? Good. Then you are feeling the rod load. Try it again.

There . . . There . . . There. . . .

Another contribution to long, flat casts is manual acceleration. You can impart greater velocity to a fly line if you take in line with your mending hand at the same instant you begin the sweep of your rod, and velocity means distance. You can achieve this effect just by anchoring your mending hand in place, say at your beltline. The cam-like action of your shoulder, casting arm, and

wrist gives the forward section of your line a little jerk as you wind up and begin to throw. That's the principle of the thing. But in order to achieve maximum velocities, you have to let your hand drift right up to the butt guides on forward and backcasts, jerking the line down sharply just at the point of loading and reversing the direction of the cast. This ultimate means of acceleration is known as the double haul, and in able hands it can drive a fly 100 feet and more.

I must back up a little bit, though. Like all things, distance casting can be overdone, can become too much of an exercise in mechanics to the exclusion of its real purpose.

With a little luck and a light tailwind, I am capable of casts to 80 feet, but the number of situations where they're called for represents about 10 percent of the time I put in troutfishing. I do think it's important to be able to put a reasonable distance between you and your target, and I would peg the average distance called for at around 40 to 50 feet.

... That's better. You're still dropping your backcast a little ... There, perfect cast! Try it again. You're a very fast learner; your line is laying arrow-straight behind you, and I can see your rod loading with power from here. Flyfishing is so damned pretty to watch; a synthesis of art and aerodynamics. You should see how that line is scribing light curves against the dark background of the stream. Get ready to shoot.

Nice! Nice snap in your wrist! You set your shoulder into a long backhaul, then rotate it forward, bending at the waist. Your shoulder, arm, and then your wrist flowed together and drove that line like a game of crack-the-whip. It shot out there pancake-flat, then barely floated down to the water. The fly touched down like a milkweed seed. You must have felt it ... like archery, right? Making a perfect cast with a fly is like hitting your target with an arrow. You know it is going to end up there the instant you release the string, and a private triumph of grace and power sweetens in your mind and your guts.

Now you're ready, at least as far as casting is concerned. Move up into position.

When casting a dry-fly to a rising fish or a station where you suspect a trout is waiting, there are three conditions that you should try to meet. Approach the trout from downstream, position yourself along the same current parallel that is bringing food to the fish, and get no closer to him than your maximum comfortable casting range.

Casting to a fish from downstream is the most reliable way to avoid spooking him by the sight of your presence, because you are working the fish from his back side. The pitch of the bed lies in your favor too, putting you a little lower in profile than if you were opposite or above the fish. This position also defines the most natural drift about 95 percent of the time: that of a free-floating fly that follows the flow of the stream unaffected by line drag.

You will find that a natural drift makes a tremendous contribution to the appeal of any fly, and positioning yourself along the same current line as the rising trout is the way to achieve this. It's nothing more than determining the patterns of movement on the surface of the stream, then getting yourself in a position to capitalize on drift lines. Identify the one that will carry your fly past the rising fish and then directly to you. It's the easiest way to avoid a fly that skates or one that is pulled down by line drag.

By maximum comfortable casting range, I mean the greatest distance you can cast without excessive effort and with a reasonable degree of accuracy. One of flyfishing's most popular myths lies within the claim that most fish are taken within 25 feet of the fisherman. This is probably true, but it is only because most fishermen are incapable of casting farther than 25 feet. If you can cast a long line, you will always catch more fish than someone who can't. It is axiomatic. Long casts keep you farther away from your fish, and allow you to reach more water.

Go ahead now. Step up into the run and wade quietly into range. I'll stay back on your off side, and watch.

You can reach the fish from where you are, so long as you hang on to your timing. Get ready to shoot the line; there's no reason for a lot of false casting unless you have to dry off a fly. Four false casts should get you 40 feet, easily.

... A perfect cast! Your line hardly made a ripple when it touched down, and the fly should float within a foot of the last rise I saw. Ed Seitz calls casts like that "stroking the water," and it is a perfect description; graceful, light, seductive. That's the way to cast a dry.

And this is the moment ... the Cahill drifts down, bristling and cocky, rotating and whirling in the shivering cross-currents. This is the finest moment in troutfishing, because you will see the fish take your duplication of nature. There is not only the feel of the strike, there is the sight of it, and the anticipation of that electric instant hones the keenest of edges. All the nerve endings are exposed when you cast a dry to a rising fish.

Just a few seconds more, and the fly will be over him. You surely mend well, facing the fly like a patient spider, pulling in

your web with your left hand while you pin it to the rod shaft with the index finger of your casting hand. Good control . . . good concentration. There is virtually no slack in the line so that you can set the hook. You don't need any lessons on mending a fly from me.

. . . There he is! Strike!

Beautiful; I saw it all! The little hump forming under the fly, the crackling flash of the rise, the line breaking free of the surface in a snap of spray. . . . Pefect timing. Keep the pressure on, the rod bent, the line taut and arrow-straight.

Careful . . . he's coming up. Watch the line.

. . . Did you see that? The way he arced over the water? I swear to you, I could see the rainbow pinpoints of sunlight in each droplet when he jumped. A beautiful brookie, 14 inches if I'm any judge.

Now he'll go deep. It's a brook trout's habit. Keep your rod tip high and line taut so you know where he is, and to keep him from getting too much of an underwater bow in the line. Did you see him zoom downstream toward you? That's the toughest trick in the book to beat . . . to strip in line fast enough to keep the pressure against the hook in his mouth. And to sidestep at the same time so he doesn't rocket between your legs. I've had fish wrap me up in line like a spider with a fly, while I did a one-legged jig trying to get untwined . . . and seized with a case of belly laughs on top of it. Nels McKenzie calls this the most fun you can have with your clothes on. He's pretty close.

The fish is tiring now. His runs have lost their zip and he's downstream, using the current to do his battle.

Strip in line slowly. Let him pump and work and tire. But be ready to release the line with your index finger to let it slip through your mending hand should he find a second wind.

There is a kind of purity about flyfishing, isn't there? It's complex some ways, yet its intermediaries are really no more than a rod, hook, and line. There are no grinding gears or click-ing bails to inject industry between the two of you, or to compensate for your own mistakes. With a fly rod, you are closest to a trout.

It's almost over now ... one more half-hearted run and he should be beat. A brook trout seldom exhibits tremendous stamina, especially after he has been jumped. He looks like he's ready for the net now; on his side, the fight gone out of him.

Just slide the rim beneath him and scoop. There! A beautiful fish, fat and well-groomed. If they're all like that in Back Brook, we have found one dream of a stream!

Admire him briefly. He's yours, and you earned him. He is pretty now, but did you ever catch one in September, when they are gaudy with mating paint? Absolutely the most strikingly beautiful trout in America. And the best eating at any time of the year.

When they're this size, I like them simple. Either fried in butter, or broiled over coals; and while they are broiling, you baste them with a sauce of white wine, butter, and sour limes. If luck is really riding on your shoulder, you might have found a few mushrooms along the stream to cook with them; boletus, or meadow mushrooms, or best of all, morels. No king ever ate a richer meal.

Do you want to keep him? It's up to you. There is no immorality in killing fish, only in wasting them. But kill him soon and quickly; a sharp blow to the head, just behind the eyes, with a thumb-thick stick will do it. It isn't just humane, a quickly-killed fish tastes better.

No? Good then. Look for signs of gill damage, and if there are none, remove the hook and hold the fish gently, facing into the current. He'll wriggle free when he recovers. By the way, I agree with you. As hot as the day is becoming, by the time we get back to the bridge his flesh will probably have lost much of its flavor and firmness, even inside the cool, canvas creel. If you had killed him you would not have had the best of him.

Now that the fish is revived and gone, you should probably take a few more test casts up into the run. That was the only trout I saw rising, but there might be another that can be coaxed to strike. It isn't worth a lot of time . . . catching a fish, especially one that jumps . . . usually puts down nearby trout for a while. Maybe three or four drifts over the spot, and then we'll look elsewhere.

So long as there isn't someone fishing ahead of you, or "beats" that are assigned or understood, you're far more likely to catch fish by covering a lot of water rather than concentrating on one fish or one station. It's a matter of probabilities. The more you confront one fish, the more likely it is that you will put him down. And by moving along, odds say that you will be casting to a variety of fish. The larger the pool of trout, the better the chance of finding one with an appetite, and it's more interesting to keep moving along. Doggedly working one place in a stream gets monotonous. When you test a station with three or four casts, then move on to the next one, your imagination and anticipation have plenty of nourishment, and the circles form more often.

No? Then move upstream to the next likely spot. As flat, wide, and gentle as Back Brook is here, I'm sure you won't get into any trouble wading right up the middle of the stream. It's probably a flat, sandy bottom, right? Then the shoreline is where the fish will be. Drop that fly right up against the banks. You've got to know where the fish are to catch them.

That's something else I think about a lot. In order to catch a trout, you've got to believe that you're going to. It helps when you see a fish rise, and to know where he is likely to be, but there's more to it: an almost metaphysical relationship that combines understanding with a sense of being plugged in . . . the idea of moving with the water. I have been fishing on days when I lost this sense. The fish were there, but something was out of sync between us. I have sometimes fought it, and eventually caught something, just to prove a personal point. But it was assertive fishing, and not at all enjoyable. So when I get that feeling I usually quit fishing and stream watch, and that has proven to be the charm. By stream watching, some sort of connection is established. Clues to the code fall into place. And the next time I go fishing, I always do much better.

You're putting yourself at a disadvantage by using that soggy fly. Unless trout are on a feeding binge, they seldom take a half-sunk dry. Part of the fault lies with my tie, I'm sure, but I'll bet you got fish slime on the fly when you unhooked the brookie. Slime is about as good a floatant as liquid dish soap.

I know of very few patterns that could be called persistent floaters, and most of them are tied with deer hair. Patterns with feather hackles and conventional bodies eventually sink, no matter how carefully I tie them. To get that fly floating high again, squeeze it in a sheet of Kleenex, then blow it back up into a fluff and dust it with the powdery fly-dry. If that doesn't work, change flies. That's why I carry so many of the same patterns.

No rises? Keep working upriver then. Just remember to cast to likely stations instead of empty water; unless, of course, you see an actively rising fish. And I think I see another, tucked in against the bank 50 yards ahead. See where that hummock of grass has fallen into the water? There's a small rotating eddy right below it. That's where I saw him.

Are you beginning to grasp how important watercraft is? Without ever looking at the spot, you know there will be a rotating eddy below the hummock, and even more important, you know the characteristics of the current lanes the eddy creates.

You did a very admirable job of covering the eddy, too. You dropped the fly right at the point of the apex, and that's a tough cast. In an eddy that small, you only have about a square foot of water for a target.

That the trout is still rising after six casts is another compliment to your touch with a fly rod, but it also suggests that you've got the wrong fly. Tell me, have you actually seen him come to the surface for a real fly? I haven't.

The easiest way to know that a fish is really taking floating flies is to track a natural fly on the water and actually see it sucked under. When three or four flies pass within two feet of a rising fish, it's a reliable sign that he's either taking tiny midges that aren't apparent to us, or that he's nymphing; striking at some insect form just under the surface.

You can also make an educated guess about what a trout is feeding on by studying the form his rise takes. A surface rise is usually more violent, often marked by the splash of a slapping tail, and with prominent ripples ringing out. Nymphing rises tend to be porpoise-like, head-to-tail rolls that create swirls rather than splashes, or raindrop dimples as the trout's back softly breaks the surface of the stream.

No, he's not nymphing. See how much water he's throwing? But I can't make out what it is he's taking. If it were midsummer, I'd say try a grasshopper as close as he is to the bank, but they're not out yet. Wait . . . I see something floating down . . . a big brown mayfly just about as dull as the surface pane. Can you grab it?

You have discovered another dimension of troutfishing that has an intrigue all its own . . . catching flies. The most practical way to do it is use the cheesecloth like a seine, either getting a floating insect to drift into it, or using it to slap one out of the air. But, human nature being what it is, you seldom go to those lengths at first. Try picking one up off the water by its wings. This requires superhuman coordination. Or letting a fly drift into the hollow of your hand. It always seems to fill up with water before he gets there and the fly detours around it. Batting one out of the air with your hat is another possibility that seldom works. When that fails, try your luck.

Sometimes, if you turn away from the wind or the current, flies will light on you of their own accord. There, see? One has perched right on your hand. A mayfly.

Fred Scholl calls mayflies one of nature's perfect marvels, but I don't think even that tribute pays them adequate homage. Those gossamer wings, the filigree along the abdomen, that fragile tail . . . their beauty rivals even butterflies and spiderwebs etched by sunlight and sprinkled with dew.

Gently now, pin its wings between your thumb and forefinger, and look at the fly's underside. This is the color the trout are seeing, and the one that must be matched. By the way, have you ever looked at a real or artificial fly from the angle it is seen by a trout, below the surface pane? Try it some time with a glass of water, or better yet, a glass-bottomed pewter mug. The surface tension which holds the fly above water, also bends light rays, and you get an impressionist's painting of an insect, not the distinct proportions and markings of a fly seen from above the water.

There . . . see the difference between the back of the thorax and abdomen and the underside? The back is oxford brown and the belly gray. Two-tone flies are common, so you can't really trust what they look like to you when they're on the water.

You will find a #12 Gray Mayfly on a flybody hook among those dry-flies. It isn't an established pattern, but something I tied that might create the impression of the real fly to a fish looking up from beneath the water. Something else . . . drop the cast above the hummock and let the fly float down the eddy fence. You've been casting into the slower eddy waters, and in that place the trout has plenty of time to look the fly over. Sometimes, you can get a trout to strike by giving him little time for careful decisions.

It doesn't look like that is the match either. That was perfectly placed, and the fish took no notice. I'd try a few more presentations, though. Sometimes you can tease a trout into striking, even if you have an off pattern. But my guess is that that trout is being super selective, and I've found fish with that attitude very hard ones to fool.

I once went so far as to carry a little attache case with a mini fly-tying kit in my car. I'd catch a fly the trout seemed to be taking, set up a bench on the hood, and do my best to imitate it.

It proved to be pretty much a waste of time. I'd say that only 10 percent of those ties took fish, and all of them were reasonably close, in size and color, to the real flies I'd caught, at least as far as I could see. My conclusion was that the trout were picking out some feature of the real fly that was not apparent to me, perhaps some illusion created by the tension of the surface pane. Whatever it was, I have never had a great deal of luck matching the hatch beyond a certain point of fish selectivity, and I don't really wish to, either. I started to get into stream entomology, but once I passed a certain point, my head rebelled. It all became too formal, technical, and head-heavy; focused on dry scholarship, instead of letting your fishing be relaxing, a little sloppy, and fun.

I have to admit that part of my feelings about stream entomology are personal, too. There is something about getting heavily into it that leads too many of us to mayfly one-upmanship; using that knowledge to intimidate, rather than to share and teach. I once guided someone like that, and to this day, I don't know why he hired me. What I remember about him most distinctly was that he considered catching a trout on a worm to be a mortal sin, and that within the first minute of our meeting, I was informed that he owned 23 cane rods and had fished for trout around the world. He could recite the latin names of every bug in a brook, chapter and verse, but he was also an intolerable bore who used his intellect like a club. The name of each insect came attached to a sense of patrician disdain, and, although he took his only delight in catching more and bigger fish than I did, I could never call him a good fisherman. He was too specialized, too narrow in his views and understanding. His real love was his learning, not a trout, and on a stream he appeared stilted and mechanical. It is the same principle that applies to music. A perfect technician is not necessarily a good musician. Machines cannot make real music, because it is the little mistakes in beat and note and timing that makes music individual, interesting, and human.

I don't mean to suggest that it's wrong to know something about the science of fishing. Putting together the web of life that surrounds a stream is part of it all. It's the priorities that I try to keep in order. If I am fishing for a trout, I want to keep him in the center of the circle. So I learned how to identify caddis, stoneflies, craneflies, mayflies, and the general look of their larvae, and left it at that.

I'm positive that fly is not the right imitation. Six casts are enough for any fish. And he hasn't risen since you changed. He might be put down. Even as well as you've been casting, you can drift a fly past a watching fish just so many times. It will likely take him 15 minutes to begin rising again . . . if at all. Perhaps he is full, or feeding on pinhead midges.

That's another path I refuse to take to a trout: coping with extraneous annoyances. When fish are rising to flies too small to see, or are so sophisticated that they demand 14-foot spiderweb leaders that snap off flies, or they are in some station that requires an extraordinary effort to reach, I'll turn to another fish or another technique. When considerations for such things as these begin to dominate my thoughts and actions, I find myself concentrating on surmounting the obstacles instead of fishing. It becomes too much of a technical battle, and the connection between fish and fisherman is broken. If you're after a trout, seek to maintain a sense of balance, too.

I haven't seen another of those big, brown flies since the one you caught. Have you?

That is another maddening thing about fishing on top. Flies blossom and bloom according to their own schedule, then disappear. You winnow out what it is the fish are taking, and just when you hit on it, they decide to switch to something else. You're left holding the bag and with the impression that you've cracked the code. But you really have to start all over again, and by the time you realize it, the cycle has turned again. There are times when I think the fish and the flies are in concert . . . a kind of mayfly conspiracy . . .

What to do now? Do you see any other rising fish? If not then the rule I follow is this: if a fish is rising regularly, try to match the fly he is taking by color, size, and general conformation. If there are no rises evident, fish a proven pattern and play your hunches.

When trout aren't rising to a specific fly, they still may strike at a pattern that rates as off the wall. Like a Royal Coachman. Now what could that represent of nature? Have you ever seen a real fly that incorporates those wild colors? Yet you will find it a great and productive fly.

It's a little like sex appeal. Some patterns have it, some don't. It's surely there, but exactly what it is is very difficult to determine. I have an idea of where it originates, though. Consider this: that at some point during the dawn of their development, trout feed on some tiny organism that no one has yet recognized, some littlest flea, infinitesimal in size, but huge in proportion to its contribution to a trout fry's diet. There could be more than one kind of these little critters too, and their color and design might well conform to a Bivisible or a Raider or some other curiously successful pattern that has no real correlate in nature. Trout would imprint and be conditioned to these patterns, just as surely as conditioned chickens learn to love an assembly of cubes and cones as their mother, and the appearance of the little bugs would ring bells. Older trout would salivate, then strike. Although this is just one possible explanation of many, if it is the answer, it creates the potential for the ultimate trout fly, some weird design or pattern that no one has yet hit upon, but that would prove irresistible. The possibility of that discovery is another little intrigue I play with while I'm fishing.

You've chosen a Hairwing Coachman. We're getting to think alike. That's just the pattern I'd have tried . . . a great floater, and trout love them. Those white wings make them easy to see, too. So long as you're fishing with hunches, you might as well pick a fly that is easy and pleasurable to work with.

We'd be better off to leave this flat water, though. Without a rise to signal a fish, there isn't much to fish to here. Back Brook takes a bend just ahead, and there's sure to be some hydraulics there. Another stream unit. Go ahead, I'll follow.

You'll probably break your leader carrying your rod that way. When you're unrigged, it's easiest to thread through this brush with it pointing behind you, the way you're holding it; but when you've got a leader and fly attached, a nub of a branch is going to hook your line and snap it, and you'll never find the fly in this tangle of roots and grass. That's it . . . hold it high and in front of you, and keep your eye on the rod tip. It's a little like fencing.

Did you ever have a grouse bust out of this kind of stuff? Suddenly there's a violent explosion at your feet, the sound of thunder, and you think you've fallen off the end of the earth. And when they rise they always seem to be heading for your throat. It always catches me off guard. It's even worse when you're creeping through snowy woods, trying to hunt a deer. The other one that draws me up short is when I step on a willow twig and it jiggles in the grass ahead. It's a real heart-stopper when you're in rattlesnake country.

Hold it . . . see that big rotating eddy on the inside of the bend? Where would you fish it from?

No, not with a dry-fly. Standing on the point bar would require a downcurrent drift to fish the eddy fence, and that's the swiftest part of the stream. I understand your thinking, but most rotating eddies are best fished from downstream. Get into the water right here, and work upcurrent.

I would make my first cast up along the eddy fence. Drop the fly just outside the place where primary and reflex currents meet, and let it drift along with the primary current. Three casts will be enough.

Next try the eddy that the reflex current has set up along the bank. That's what you were thinking about, right? That trout stationed there would be looking away from you if you approached him from the point bar.

You're quite right, but you can also handle 50 feet of line, and that should be enough distance to prevent any fish from seeing you, even at high noon when the sun's angle of incidence to the water is at its most revealing.

The other rule you're breaking, with cause, is that you are really fishing a dry downcurrent when you work the inside of a rotating eddy from this position in the stream, but a downcurrent drift holds reasonable potential so long as the current is moving very slowly. The test is simple. If your fly skates or sinks, forget a downcurrent cast. The water is too swift for a decent presentation.

If the fish wanted that fly, you would have had your strike. That drift was so pretty, and the fly rode so high, that it made *me* want to grab it! Don't forget the apex of the eddy where the current is impelled. That's one of the hottest spots in a stream.

Well done, right on the button! It's that sort of presentation that makes fishing nearly as much fun to watch as to do. But no one seems to be home, or if they are, they aren't hungry.

Now there's another technical problem for you: the bank eddy across-current. The feasibility of a cross-current cast is pegged to the same factor as for a downcurrent cast, the speed of the water. The faster the flow, the closer must be the angle of your cast to current lines. If you exceed this maximum angle, the current will grab and bow your line, and pop your fly around like a bass bug.

The first thing to do is get downriver of your target, and as far away as your cast can comfortably reach. See how being able to handle a long line comes in handy? Now from that position, imagine a line drawn between you and your target, meeting another line that follows your current lane. This defines the angle of your cast. It looks like about 45 degrees, and the speed of the water as it runs by the bank is about four miles per hour. You will find it's a little too fast to pull off a natural drift.

But you can often buy time for the current's effect by making a slightly longer cast than is necessary to reach your target, then drawing the cast up short by snubbing the line. It creates an elastic effect, whereby the line recoils in the air and settles on the water in a series of gentle Ss. Since the water between you is moving faster than the bank eddy ahead, it takes time for all the kinks to work out, and for the line to straighten. Keep all the slack that forms at your rod tip stripped in, or you won't be able to set the hook. Should a fish strike the second the fly settles, strike back very hard. There will be about six feet of slack when you snub a 40-foot cast.

Not bad! See how that little trick works? Actually, I only use it when I am working to a rising fish. Random casting in fast water with a dry gets to be another extraneous annoyance; about half the time I don't snub the line enough and the fly sinks, and it's a race to mend line. But it's a handy thing to know when you have a hot fish across a swift current.

Don't work that eddy for too long. Two, maybe three quick drifts are all you'll need. It seems like the fish aren't exactly in a frenzy over feeding; high noon is kind of a poor time to fish anyway. So move upstream, and cover a lot of water fast. This is an especially good time of day to fish shadows on the water.

Back Brook gets shallow again above this bend, so wade up the middle of the bed, banging away at any possible station within reach of your casts; sweepers, sleepers, eddies. Rather than long, seductive drifts that require a lot of mending, try short floats that require manipulating no more than six feet of line.

It is a kind of a physically satisfying way to fish, full of vibrant activity, and an exercise in accuracy and handling line. Working over rising fish is deliberate and seductive. Casting at probabilities hums like a well-oiled machine.

How long should you keep it up? As long as it feels good to you. If, after 10 minutes or so, the Coachman gets no strikes, change to another pattern, and another. But you've been fishing on top for 45 minutes so far, and haven't seen a recent rise or had a strike since that last fish.

That doesn't necessarily suggest that the fish are not biting, only that they are not biting on top. If you are insistent about taking a trout on a dry-fly, go ahead, fish upriver some more. But if conditions remain as they are, I'll bet you won't catch a thing, and that you'll soon tire of the whole business. You'll remember that the lawn has to be mowed, or that you have a dinner date at seven with the Groids, whom you detest, and you'll quit fishing to entertain those dreary pastimes.

On the other hand, remember that surface forms represent only about 15 percent of a trout's diet. The other 85 percent of the time, they're feeding on the bottom. So if you really want to catch a trout, the next step is to try nymphs.

No . . . go ahead, take a few more casts to give fish and fate just one more chance. From a probable point of view, dry-flies are always a long shot, but they are so much fun that it's worth challenging the odds. Then let's take a break here on the bank. You'll have to change spools on the Hardy, to the sinking tip line. I haven't seen one nymphing rise in the quarter-mile or so of Back Brook that we've fished, so we'll fish deep. There's a rule to commit to memory, too. If there is no surface activity what-soever, fish as close to the bottom as your skills and equipment will allow. That's where the fish will be looking for food, if, indeed, they are feeding at all.

Your legs are probably tired and cold after bucking that current too. I know mine are, just from the balancing I had to do getting over logs and tippy boulders. Besides, in your persistent pursuit of a trout, you probably haven't noticed that the wild roses are in bloom. Stretch out here in the sun, and let it soak up the wet spots on your waders while you take a whiff of that rose smell. It and the scent of young, succulent grass have been coming up around me in sweet, clean waves that float like mirages. Troutfishing isn't all work.

And hear that meadowlark and the chatter of blackbirds? How much better could this day be?

I've been thinking about this stream and why you aren't catch-ing as many fish as it tells me you should. One possibility is that this isn't the right time for Back Brook. Every place has its own personality, it's own rhythms, and part of them is a period of time when the fishing is especially good and another when its especially bad. I can't say why, but this is a pretty universal trait.

A wild rose

Nor can I suggest any formula for predicting what body of water will be hot at what time. It's the kind of knowledge you get from trial and error and a lot of fishing, but extremely profitable information to have.

For example, I've come to know that Milkshake Lake is the place to go for the first month of the season. Cutthroat and grayling bank up around the lake's inlet, and go crazy for a little fly that I tie with a cream body, orange underside, and grizzly hackle. It's the only place and time when that fly works well, but it's not unusual to catch 30 fish in a morning on it. Then, Milkshake dies. It's absolutely terrible fishing for the rest of the season, but toward the last week of that first month, the Roaring River comes on strong to lures and bait. That lasts about two weeks, then Quicksilver Creek and the Beaver Ponds bust open for dry-flies. No exaggeration, I have taken 162 fish in a day from the Beaver Ponds during this period. The first day that Sil ever cast a dry-fly, she took 17 trout in 21 casts there. And the fishing holds up like that well into September. But Lagoon Lake enters my patterns long before then; about the middle of July. Great logs of browns and rainbows start cruising the weedy flats, and they like gold spoons and Goofus Bugs. The Gunflint comes on like gangbusters to a dry Royal Coachman around the first of August, and the Goldfish Bowl is superb for flies when the streams elsewhere are high, roily, and fishable only with bait.

I can't tell you any easy way to learn such secrets about Back Brook. You'll have to pay your dues first. But there will be some little quirk to this river, that, once understood, will open it up to you. Look for the clues under every rock, and you will eventually understand its moods, and why trout fishing is always best when you know a body of water intimately. Always fish in places that feel friendly.

Ready to move on already? You're an eager fisherman, I'll give you that. Let's go then, and see what they'll do with a nymph today.

7 / *There Is a Beautiful Nymph by That Rock*

Take these two willow snags and roll them in the edges of the cheesecloth so you can hold it open. It's a little bit easier to seine with two people, but there will be times you'll have to seine alone, so you might as well learn the technique that way.

Because any clues about nymphing activity will be below the surface, it's practically a prerequisite to nymph fishing that you seine the water before making a choice of a fly.

If you forget the cheesecloth, turning over a rock is second best, but if won't reveal any insects that are free-floating. If they're in the stream, they're likely to be the trout's favorite menu. Nor will it reveal those insects that dislodge and float away as you pick the rock up. These are the next most likely candidates to imitate. All you'll find are the most tenacious and best hidden of a stream's nymphal inhabitants. They are at least an assurance that by using a closely similar imitation you'll have something that fits into the natural scheme of the stream, but that's not really a lot to go on. Trout feed more in response to the availability of food in a stream than in response to hunger. We tend to say, "they're not biting," or "they're not hungry," but what's really happening is that there's no natural food around to key their feeding instincts. "Off feed" is really a more precise term, and when they are off, you can drift a fly, a lure, or a worm right by their noses and they won't take it. Even if a perfectly natural bait drifted into their mouth, a worm that blundered into the water or a nymph that lost its grip on a rock, they'd probably spit it out.

Then something happens that starts funneling food into the water. Not just a chance morsel, but a pattern the trout can recognize, that is a natural consequence of some change in the environment. Say the surface pane is shattered by a heavy rain, and then worms start to show up. Or the stream temperature rises, and nymphs start floating down. Trout still don't exactly

Stonefly nymph

get hungry, but they see it's time to eat . . . there's an important difference. So they go on feed, and you can then catch them, so long as your hook is dressed with something that fits into the pattern they see.

You look doubtful. Then how about this? If trout were capable of recognizing hunger, it would follow that they would also stop eating when they get full. When they are on feed, however, they gorge themselves to the point that when they open their mouths, they lose more food from the pressure of their distended stomachs than they can take in, and yet they will still strike a hook. I have also snagged trout on days when they "weren't biting." It was obvious that my hook was close enough for them to have seen it, but they didn't strike at it, and such fish invariably had empty stomachs without a speck of food in them. Something else about those days: when I seined the water, I came up with absolutely nothing tumbling down. The only food around was my single contribution, and it was hardly a pattern that a trout could identify.

So that seine can be a very important little item to carry around with you, a test not just for what they might be biting on, but whether they're biting at all.

Take it then, and go into the water . . . the shallow riffle coming off the upstream side of this point bar. That's always the place to start, in a riffle. If nymphs are in the water, that's where they'll be coming from.

You don't have to go far from shore . . . calf deep is plenty. Now face upstream and stretch the opened seine before you. That way you'll collect free-floating nymphs rather than those you might dislodge with your feet. Insects should turn up within two minutes of seining, and if they do, we might have to change back to a floating line, especially if they are small, say the size of a #16 hook and under. They would then be floating well up off the bottom, and trout would look for them high. But I'll bet you don't get any. When trout are taking that size nymph you always see a few swirls.

Nothing? I was afraid of that. Try seining deeper then, at knee-to-thigh depths, and get in a current lane. It will be carrying all the natural foods from the riffles above, and maybe even a few terrestrials.

Clean? We are really playing hell to make wages today. Alright, come on back to the riffle. You'll have to kick rocks.

Face downstream with the seine in front of you and tight against the bottom. Jiggle the rocks at your feet. Try not to kick them loose or turn them over, just shake them up a bit. Wait for the sediment to settle . . . now let's see what you've caught.

Beautiful, aren't they? Only a trout fisherman would use a seductive word like "nymph" to describe these insects. To most straight-thinking people, "nymph" suggests the White Rock Girl, Nabokov's coy little Lolitas, or the woodland fairies of mythology. To us, it means something with crab legs, armor plating, and jaws that snap sideways. Nymphs aren't the only confusing items that appear to have become the trout fisherman's legacy, though. Ever hear the term "damsel fly?" It's as suggestive as "nymph," but it describes a close cousin of the dragonfly. I have, however, run into one piece of common sense. In the West, baitfishermen call nymphs "scratchers." Good, hard-headed, practical fishermen, Westerners.

I'll tell you something else, it might not be at its best today, but this really is a fertile stream. There must be two-dozen insects in that seine. No, I don't know the names of each species, but I can tell you a few things about families.

That one right there, crawling up toward the rim of the seine, eventually becomes a mayfly. There must be a hundred different kinds of mayflies, but you can always tell the family because the nymph looks like a cross between a crab, a spider, and a scorpion.

And this soft, segmented, caterpillar-like worm is a cranefly larva. You've seen the adults, I'm sure. They look like huge mosquitoes, with crane legs, but actually, they prey on mosquitoes.

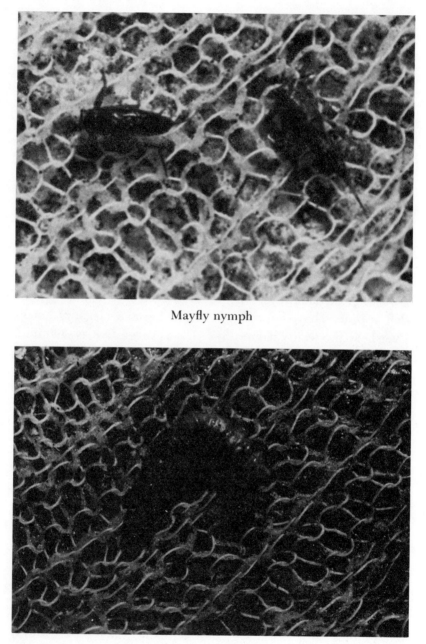

Mayfly nymph

Cranefly nymph

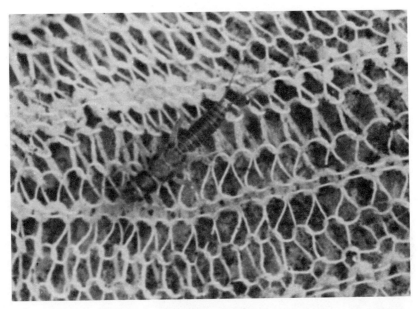

Stonefly nymph

Caddis on rock

This fierce-looking critter with a football-shaped abdomen and bulbous eyes that take up half its head is a dragonfly nymph. You can also tell them by the tiny wingbutts sticking out of the top of their thorax. And this tawny nymph with antennae, two slender tails, and a long, segmented abdomen, will eventually turn into a stonefly.

Caddis? No, I don't see any in the seine, but I can show you one form very easily. Just reach down and pick up one of those rocks you were kicking around. See those little cones of pebble and twig attached to the underside? Those are the stick-houses of caddis larvae. The insect builds that case for protection, and it works pretty well. No caddis larvae turned up in the seine, did they?

It's obvious that one species predominates, though . . . that tawny brown scratcher that looks like it can bite from both ends. Hand it to me, will you? C'mon . . . pick it up. It won't bite.

My nymph box holds a pretty close partner; a #10 Stonefly, with the same pale yellow underside.

I can be better persuaded of the need to match real nymphs to mirror artificials than real adults and dries. A fly underwater is much clearer in color and detail to a fish than one floating on the surface. But the variety of nymphs present in a stream is vast, and the limits of my nymph box small by comparison, so I often fish the closest approximation rather than a perfect imitation. Contrary to my logic, I haven't noticed any dramatic difference between the two in catch power. Like dries, so long as the fly is the right overall color and size, it will interest enough trout to interest you.

Now that you have winnowed out the closest look-alike you have available, scoop up some water in your hand and give the fly a good dunking. Depending on the tying materials used, colors may changes when the fly is wet, so compare it to its natural counterpart again.

The size of the nymph pattern I choose is critical to whether or not I weight the nymph. If all signs point to bottom-feeding fish, I'll choose a weighted nymph if the imitation I'm using is larger than a #8. I've observed that real nymphs float very close to the bottom when they're big, and that large, unweighted imitations don't. They have too many neutral-buoyancy body materials in relation to the weight of the hook; so the larger the fly, the heavier the weighting I wind under the body. You can also duplicate the performance of a weighted fly by pinching a small shot 6 inches ahead of the hook; but in either case, realize that you have created something of a monster when you weight a fly heavily.

The mechanics of flyfishing do not lend themselves to casting any sort of weight, and doing so is awkward; another of those intruding petty annoyances that I'd rather avoid. It can also be painful. The weight on the end of the leader whirls like a bolo in the air, and should it drift to your off side on a forward cast, it will hit your head a clout that will make your eyes tear. I once had a teacher who delighted in sneaking up behind anyone who wasn't doing what he considered correct, and cracking them behind the ear with his knuckle. Every time I get hit with a shot, that SOB flickers to mind. The weight also drops your backcast, which limits range, and may also give your fishing partner a heart attack. One day, while fishing the Gunflint with Dick Weden, I happened to hook the cloth of his jacket on a heavily-weighted nymph. I heard the cry of a man in mortal fear of his life as my forward cast stopped dead. My first worry was that I'd hooked him either in the eyelid or private parts, but as it turned out, Dick's real fear was of rattlesnakes, and he thought he'd been snakebit.

It would have been some acrobat of a rattlesnake that could strike a forearm from a swimming position in the middle of a swift stream, but pointing that out didn't calm Dick a bit.

Now that we're done with them, clean off the net and put the nymphs back in the stream. It preserves the energy cycle of the ecosystem, and it might set you up a chumline. I'll stretch the net across these bleached rocks and it will dry in a minute. In the meanwhile, you might take a cast or two down into the rotating eddy and across to the bank eddy where you fished the dry. Nothing elaborate, just drift the nymph down along the eddy fence, and let it wash around the dead water where the currents realign themselves.

I've caught trout by fishing a nymph downstream, but it isn't my favorite technique. It reminds me of trolling. Not that I have anything against trolling, just that it is less exciting and absorbing than other ways of fishing.

Something else that may work against you: when you wade downstream, you create quite a bit of commotion, stirring up the stream bed, and pieces of sediment drift ahead of you. There are two sides to this argument; one says that you stir up bait, which improves the fishing, and the other, that the unnatural, sudden clouding of the water alerts trout that something is out of order. I tend to hold with the latter, especially on days like today when the fish are finicky and down. I've watched trout fin in clear, sunwashed runs from a high bank, and they react immediately to anything different . . . a wrist-thick beaver cutting drifting down, the shadow of a kingfisher sizzling along . . . they scoot into hiding faster than the eye can see. So perhaps it would be wiser to leave this place and work upstream again. Casting a nymph upcurrent corresponds more closely to fact.

If they are capable of swimming, nymphs do so very slowly. When they are swept or sucked from under a rock, they are largely at the mercy of currents, tumbling downriver at the speed of the current that has captured them. This is a difficult, if not impossible drift to achieve with a fly when you're working downriver. The relationship between current and caster implies either lateral movement of the bait, no movement at all in relation to the bottom, or a nymph breasting the flood as you strip in line. It never happens in real life.

I suspect fish are like humans in a few respects, one of them being that the relative intelligence of members of the species is reflected in a bell-shaped curve that reaches its population peak at the 100 IQ mark. In other words, there are as many dumb trout as there are smart trout, and downriver nymphing probably fools the dumb ones. But the element of a natural drift is sure to fool dumb ones, and it collects a few smart ones that would never otherwise fall for such a patent fake as a caddis worm or cranefly larva swimming upstream. Upriver nymphing also puts the fly closer to the bottom, where fish are accustomed to look for it.

I also prefer to fish a nymph in slightly faster water than what I would call ideal for a dry ... currents around four miles an hour. In this case, the horse followed the cart. It gradually became apparent that I was catching more fish in the faster water, so I began fishing there more often, and it has become a habit. I have a feeling that it is more productive because trout don't have a lot of time to look the fly over.

This is the kind of place I would pick to start; a broad, shallow riffle tumbling into a swift run. I've found nymphs very appealing when fished off a riffle.

Pick a target ... try the midpoint of the riffle bar, where it drops off into deep water. Get close enough to reach it with a cast. Your position in relation to flow lines is identical to the one you would assume with a dry-fly. Line up the flow lines so that the fly would drift into your hip pocket.

Fishing a nymph on a dead drift, is less exacting sport than dry-fly fishing. Still, correctly interpreting bottom structure, and reading lines of flow, remain the foundations on which this house is built. You continue to cast upcurrent to likely stations from positions on the same current parallel as when you fish a dry, but if you hit the outside rather than the inside of an eddy fence, or the current gets ahead of you and begins to draw the fly out of the calm waters of an eddy, the effect on appeal isn't quite so critical as when a dry-fly starts to skate across the surface. But what nymphing relinquishes in precision casting, it takes back in other demands.

The most difficult trick to master is identifying a take. As the current brings the line back to you, it is virtually impossible to keep sufficient slack out of the line to feel the tug of a mouthing trout. They suck at a nymph, then drop it in an instant, and are gone long before the act of stripping in line puts the two of you in touch. Nor are they likely to hook themselves, because there is no line drag.

In order to spot a take on a dead drift, you have to watch your line as it floats down toward you. The instant it stops, you must strike and set the hook. It is not an easy technique to master, because watching fly line on the move is like trying to pick out a spot on telephone wire as you whiz along at 60 miles per hour. Instead of a stationary object, you see an undulating line. But the effect is negated when you reach a reference point ... a telephone pole.

You can make a reference point ... or points ... on sinking line, by painting inch-long sections of it with red or fluorescent orange nail polish or airplane dope at 3-foot intervals.

If you're fishing with floating line, an even better trick is to whip a thin length of fluorescent orange wool at the very tip. Creating a reference point in this manner isn't the whole answer ... you still have to be able to see the relationship of the line to the surface pane. But it at least simplifies the learning.

There is no easy way to accustom your eyes to this relationship. It's a craft that comes with practice.

Competence lies in the ability to perceive the whole picture, rather than individual parts. Human beings tend to be locked into one-track looking. You watch your line, and ignore its relationship to the moving water, or you concentrate on the water and lose your lock on a specific point on your line. A fish strikes, and by the time you realize the relationship between the line and water has changed, the trout is gone and grinning.

Instead of looking at one spot, try to concentrate on line and water at once ... the night vision trick again. Seeing that relationship is a close relative of reading water.

Nice cast! Flat and straight. That weight-forward sinking line really lays it out there, doesn't it? Now as the line drifts back toward you, strip it in just fast enough to keep a deep bend from forming under your rod tip. That's another reference point you can use. A little jump in that part of your line signals a strike.

Keep stripping . . . keep stripping. . . . mend that line right up to the leader butt. Trout often follow a nymph before they take it, and sometimes they'll have second thoughts about the food that just went by, race out of their station, and grab it toward the end of the drift. That sink-tip line dictates a long, nearly complete mend anyway. Deep-running line won't break loose of the water like floating line, and the problem is compounded because the current is bringing the line to you. When you pick up a sinking line on a dead drift, it really helps if you'll haul right from the butt guide to get some extra acceleration.

That mend is fine for this kind of fishing . . . the same one used for a dry. Drawing line in with one hand while you pin it to the shaft with your index finger is the only way to keep up with a fast-drifting line, and you can strike one-handed. But you're going to have to do something with those loose strands of mended line drifting around your legs. In flat water, you can let it float, but in this faster water, the current twists, turns, and sinks it. If it doesn't birds-nest you, it will cut down on your casting range, because the inertia of the cast line will be wasted on pulling the mended line out of the water.

There, see? You couldn't shoot out your full line. You lost six or seven feet of distance tearing loose from the surface. On a short cast of 40 feet or under, grasp the line just like you've been doing, and draw it a full arm's length, but instead of dropping it to the stream, let it form a loose coil in the palm of your mending hand as it returns for another draw.

On a long cast, you'll find that a substantial amount of line will build up in your hand by the time the drift is complete. When you cast again, the loose coils of line will foul each other unless you alternate their size. The easiest way to engineer staggered loops is make one coil out of two draw-lengths of line, then make the next coil out of one draw-length.

You've worked that place long enough. Wade up another 20 feet and cast again. Three or four drifts will cover the rest of the water.

Pretty cast! It's much easier to shoot those coils out there when they're in your hand. The line sang through your guides like a silk whistle, and the fly plunked down soft as a raindrop.

Now draw in line; smooth, long strokes. Form the coils as they fall in your palm. Cast again to a spot where you know a fish will be. Concentrate on him; you know he's down there, finning close to the bottom with baleful eyes and gills slowly pumping. Get connected to him . . . sometimes you can actually psych a trout into biting.

There it is! Strike!

Dammit, I thought you had one. Snag. But that's alright, a good thing, in fact. You can see that little pause in your line, and you're getting down deep. Can you rollcast?

If you put a sharp roll in the line and snap it up to the fly, that will usually pop it free. If that trick doesn't work, you'll have to wade upstream of the snag and tug it loose from that direction. Don't worry about putting fish down. You've made ten casts to the riffle, by my count, and that's a sufficient test of trout interest. Probably of yours, too.

Do you find upstream nymph fishing a little wearying? It's somewhat less enjoyable than dry-flyfishing, partly because of that line. You must concentrate on it at the cost of other things, and that excludes a lot of little pleasures. With a dry there is always the fascination of a little boy with a toy boat; small rushes of excitement and gentle currents of satisfaction as it whirls and dips and floats along. You see vignettes of bank, reflection, eddy, and rock. With a nymph, there's really nothing to watch except the monotonous line.

Now that you're free, cast to another station. There's a gentle two-dimensional eddy just above you. I'd try it. And you don't have to jockey around so much as with a dry. You can't angle too far away from flow lines, but you don't have to be so perfectly aligned with them, either.

Because an absolutely free drift is not essential to nymph fishing, I tend to cast them to every conceivable station—before as well as behind surges and two-dimensional eddies. If I have a sinking line, I'll also test the bottom of deep pools. Other places worth a casual cast where I don't normally fish a dry include the race that forms as streams enter deep, sharp meanders and channels in the river bed.

You'll find some places are too swift for nymphing, though. It's an easy test. When you have trouble keeping up with an incoming line, when the bend of line between rod tip and water begins to belly deeply and you can't keep the belly out, move on to softer water.

My compliments, by the way. You are getting very good with that fly rod; able to handle 50 feet of line now, and with authority. I've seen that nymph home in on just the right places; the fence along that two-dimensional eddy, the little surge on your left, and the rotating eddy by the roots of that old cottonwood. You are reading water well, too. But you haven't had any strikes on that Stonefly nymph, and you surely put it in front of some trout, so I'd suggest changing flies. Try something outrageous and illogical this time.

For all our careful efforts to approximate nature, she has a habit of laughing in our faces, so let's laugh right back. Use something big and whimsical. There is even a kind of logic behind this illogic.

Ever hear of Big Spring Creek? It is "flyfishing only" water, and the trout there are incredibly sophisticated. Number 20 dries and nymphs, and 14-foot leaders, are the only things that will fool them, and more often than not, they will swim up to a drifting mite of a fly, look it over like a jeweler appraising a diamond, and refuse it in a swirl of contempt. These fish are not just smart, they are aristocratic snobs, and intimidating as hell.

But just the other day, Ed St. Cin went over there, and after fishing the obligatory #20's in front of those damnable trout, he threw up his hands in exasperation, tied on The Fly Least Likely to Succeed, and committed himself to casting practice. He cleaned house. Twenty trout in a morning; the largest, a brown trout of 4½ pounds, a fish of bulk and breeding that is universally viewed as the smartest Salmo that swims. And do you know what fly Ed was using? A #6 green Wooly Worm!

Crazy luck? A one-in-a-million long shot? I don't know about that. The place I cut my teeth as a fly fisherman was a small pond that was an abandoned cranberry bog. When it wasn't used to grow berries anymore, a trout hatchery bought the place. It too, eventually was abandoned, but a stock remained; residue fish that either escaped or were overlooked during the last roundup. They survived, and reproduced, and eventually reverted to as natural a brook trout as I have seen anywhere, with olive and brown vermiculations as distinctive as etchings, and fire-red spots, surrounded by aureoles of electric blue.

Their existence was known to quite a few locals, and their wild nature put a premium on their heads, as virtually every other trout-supporting water around was stocked to the gills with hatchery fish. Predictably, the brookies received steady fishing pressure with worms and lures, these two techniques widely known to be far more effective than flies.

And that is how I fished the pond too, until the sun stretched out and began to race across the sky. Then I'd get my fly rod and practice casting for an hour. One day, just by chance, I hooked a trout on my practice fly. It was a Gentry wet. I thought it was a mistake until I hooked another. And then another.

I fished the pond with flies from that day forward, on off hours, when no one was around, or hidden way in the back where the mudholes and bogs made for footing too treacherous for more casual anglers, and did I catch fish! . . . Six, sometimes seven pan-sized brookies a day! I can still remember the best day, at least by the month and catch. One morning in May, I netted 13 fish, and four of them were between 11 and 14 inches.

There are parallels to be drawn from both Big Spring Creek and Mill Pond. The most important is that the trout in them fell to something different, something unassociated with fishermen. I am positive that those browns in Big Spring Creek saw that fat Wooly Worm go by and said something like, "Harry . . . did you see that? I haven't had a meal like that in years. Day in, day out they feed me like a bird. No fisherman could ever be attached to that!" So he struck. The brookies in Mill Pond had learned to be wary of worms and lures, but flies were "safe" because they were something different. You can carry this further, too. I have no doubt that worms and lures would clean up on "flyfishing only" waters, not because they are inherently more appealing, but because they would represent a natural food that in smell and appearance is never a part of the "fisherman threat." Similarly, if "worm fishing only" waters were legislated into being and fly-fishermen poached there, they would have the advantage. That's another reason why I don't like to fish in such specially-regulated places; they don't require trout to bend their every instinct to survival, or you to use your ingenuity. Catching them is not the sport that it could be.

Whether you agree with that or not, accept the principle as valid; experimenting with the offbeat can spring a stream loose. About the only guidelines I begin with when picking an offbeat fly involve color. If I have killed a trout, I look at the overall shade of his stomach contents and pick a fly with a similar hue. Lacking that kind of input, I use the color of the water as a guide. If the water appears brownish in deep holes, I will choose a brown fly, if it is greenish, a green fly, and so forth.

So survey the nymph box once again, and play a hunch. Good choice! A big, green Wooly Worm. You've picked the most ubiquitous fly of all the nymph patterns . . . about as good under-water as a Royal Coachman is on top.

There's a big sweeper ahead . . . jutting half in and half out of the water . . . looks like a blown down Douglas fir. The eddy below it hugs the bank for 20 feet. When you get that knot tied, drop a cast right along the fence, and we'll see what luck this new fly brings.

There is something especially attractive about a sweeper to

me when I'm flyfishing. I don't know what it is . . . logically, there are more probable hydraulics for holding a trout. But sweepers are the most inviting to work over. Perhaps it's their visual balance. The pocket of water behind them would be a favorite place of mine if I were a trout. I like the calmness of sweepers, and the sound of the little, breaking wave where log joins water. Their composition is rich too; wood, earthen bank, and water.

Perfect! You dropped it not 3 inches from the log. Now mend that line smoothly so it barely snakes toward you.

There he is! Nice fish! A head-shaker the way the shaft pulses. You can always tell a heavy trout by that. When you first hook them they pump and yank. They're shaking their head from side to side, trying to spit out the hook. Hang on . . . he'll run in an instant. The place where you took him and the way he's fighting, I'd lay odds he's a big brown, and they really have the power.

He knows he's hooked now. Look at the line cut the water! When he's strong enough to tow that thick line so fast that it hums, you know you're into a fine fish.

Watch it. He's heading downstream and if he gets into the swift water you'll have the power of it and him to contend with.

That's it . . . a little more pressure . . .

You've lost him!

How did that happen? In no way were you horsing the fish. You played him perfectly, maybe even underplayed him a little. Let me see where he broke off.

There's your answer. See that little curl on the very end of the broken tippet? Probably a wind knot; just a simple overhand that wound itself in there as the fly turned over, but the bend in the knot was so sharp that the line cut itself when it was stressed. That's why fishing knots all have multiple twists. The wraps of line cushion instead of cut.

I should have warned you about that, but checking for wind knots is so natural to me that I didn't think of you. You can get by with them when they are up toward the thick part of the leader, but when they're close to the fly they cut line strength in half. Another thing I should have told you was to check the line after you caught that brookie. They have a habit of twisting themselves up in a leader, and sometimes they nick the line with their teeth.

Too bad. A fish that size would have been supper for you. Poached in wine with a garnish of tomatoes, onions, and a pat or two of butter, even big fish like that come through with a delicate flavor. If it's any consolation, consider that you remember the fish you lose more than those you land. It was a big fish, but it will get bigger in your mind as the day goes on; when they get away, they're always a record.

So the only real loss was the fly, and I can turn them out eight to the hour. That's another beauty of the Wooly Worm; you can tie it with two left thumbs.

Besides, a take on the first cast with a new fly is like Manna from Heaven. We might have finally hit upon what's turning them on. Knot on a new tippet and another Wooly Worm. There are trout to be caught, and it looks like we've got what it takes.

8 / *Lake Trout*

I'm getting the feeling that fish was a fluke.

... Somehow I knew you were going to say that the moment the word left my mouth. Perhaps I'm getting to know you? Don't worry; anybody who would dare to make such a terrible pun at least has a sense of humor. It helps when the fish are off feed.

We covered some prime water for a nymph back there; deep and dark and swift, rushing around big, angular boulders. A very different game from those meadow meanders, with their flat water.

Back Brook seems to be changing its nature again. The pine and fir are closing in, and the bed is pitching upward. The stream is adjusting for some kind of irregularity above here. I can tell by the look of the place.

But in one way, it's the same as below. See the riffle-pool relationship? The water right here is swift and white and shallow, but above us the stream is dark again. The relationship is a

little harder to see; the dark water is swift, and there isn't a pronounced widening of the bed into a run or a pool, but it's there, the same response of the streambed to water on the move.

These bed contours and the pitch are more in tune with spinning gear, but I do see one probable place to cast a fly. That big boulder in the middle of the dark water. The quiet water, the fly water, lies between the two tailing waves that curl off the edge of the boulder.

You'll have to work over to a point directly downstream of the pocket. That's some pretty swift water, so you won't be able to hedge on lines of flow, not even if you snub your cast.

There's a strong possibility you won't be able to reach that position, by the way. The depth and swiftness of the water here make for dangerous wading. That's because as you wade deeper, you become more buoyant and less firmly attached by gravity to the rocks beneath your feet. It was a charming pleasantry back at the bridge, but when you add the power of a heavy current, you're asking to be swept off your feet.

No ... better not go further. You're unstable and hobbling, with water curling around your knees. Forget fishing the eddy, it's not worth the risk; crab your way back to shore.

Violent two-dimensional eddies aren't very good for flyfishing anyway, and you're getting into another of those extraneous annoyances where you have to focus on overcoming difficulties instead of fish. Besides, I'm sure we'll find better fly water by following this path. It detours around the rapids, and the lay of the land has a lot in common with the canyon below Mountain-gate. There might be a lake up here somewhere, too. At least more flat water. It's this hill we've been climbing. The path dished up gently at first, but it's gaining altitude fast. The valley walls say something too. Do you see how they are wide and U-shaped, rather than meeting at a sharp V? It's a dependable sign that there was a glacier here once. I'll bet that if you climbed up to one of those rock faces, you'd find scrape marks. As they move down a valley, glaciers carry rocks and boulders locked in their ice, and these grind and scrape against the valley walls as the ice moves downslope. It's quite common to find those scars exposed today, even though they were made a million years ago.

Notice how the trail is flattening out? Put that together with the shape of the valley, and this mound of earth we've been climbing begins to look like a moraine, the enormous pile of rubble a glacier pushes before it, like a colossal bulldozer. When the glacier melts away, this moraine remains, acting like a plug that dams the valley behind it.

And there's the lake that it created. Look at it, down through the pines. There's always a sense of infinite peace when you come upon a glacial lake. The streams below it are always swift; you become conditioned to their white noise and the heaving, changing patterns of busy water. Then you come to the lake and a still, reflective atmosphere settles over your shoulders, light as a down quilt on a chilly night. A mountain lake is a kind of oasis; inviting, serene, almost foreign in it's tranquility. . . .

Another bit of luck! Do you see that boat pulled up in the grass? An old, livery rowboat! I haven't seen one of them in

years. My grandfather used to take me fishing in one of those. No noise, no smoke, just the lazy creak and comfortable splash of oars. What great boats they were to fish from!

They have incredible carry, too. Just one strong sweep of the oars and they'll go and go and go, like a canoe, but even prettier. It's the stern that makes them so pretty; that graceful upsweep from the skeg, and the canted transom, like an old sailing ship. Talk about memories!

And look at the oars. Real straight-grained oak. They feel so good in your hand, like being wired to the water. It's been a long time, but we used to catch some trout from an old relic like this.

Say . . . would you mind if I rowed along the shore? There's hardly a ripple on the water, and without a wind, I'll bet I could go around the lake in 15 minutes. Wait until you see the clean wake these things cut. They make a modern outboard look like a bathtub.

. . . No, hop in. There's a good chance we'll catch some fish. In a lot of ways, lakes are even better than streams for troutfishing, and I see swallows swooping low over the water. That's one of those little things that might signal a big change. When insect-eating birds are over water, it means there are insects there. Swallows. . . . Ha! Did you ever hook one while you were false casting, or better yet, a bat? One of troutfishing's more surprising moments. Bats are especially unnerving. You don't really know if you want your fly back, and they're not heavy enough to snap your leader.

Just cast out the stern. The way things look, you've got the best bait for a lake right now. If you don't see rises on a calm lake, you know they're not taking dries. A big nymph like that Wooly Worm is as good a choice as any.

Just sit in the stern and troll. I'd strip off a little more line than you've been casting. Getting a lot of distance between you and your fish is important in a lake. You should also tug on the line with your mending hand. Just short, sharp jerks. There isn't any current to add life to your fly, and those tugs make the feather fibers on the Wooly Worm lay back and then fan out. It seems to interest trout more.

Something else I've noticed about trolling in a lake. Whether you're using a fly or a lure, an extraordinary number of strikes come as you're making a turn. I think it's because fish assume the bait is trying to get away, and it triggers some predatory mechanism in a trout.

That's good; just short, rapid tugs. I'll zig-zag us along close to shore. We don't really have the time or equipment to look for structure or current lanes, so that's that next most logical place to fish . . . within casting distance of shore.

Lake fishing is really pretty simple sport when you compare it to the technical problems you face in water on the move, but in a way, that's what's so pleasurable about it. It is as tranquil as the lake itself; quiet and relaxing. Don't get the impression that tranquility implies less action from the fish, though. A very fertile lake will support two-and-a-half times the amount of trout that a fertile stream will, primarily because of the energy they conserve when they don't have to contend with moving water.

Trout that live in lakes are, on the average, larger, too, for basically the same reasons, and there is a special thrill when you hook into a heavy fish in still water. You can really feel him work. There's no current to help you or him, and there are no limits set by banks. He goes where he wants to go, and every time he makes a searing run, to who knows where, your heart gets caught in your tonsils. There is a unique kind of purity in lake fishing, too. One that you don't find on a stream. I'm not saying it's better, just different, and there are times when I really enjoy the change.

But do you know what I like best of all about lake fishing? What we are doing right now. Not the trolling alone, but its utter simplicity. This is one place you can take a kid or a great-grandmother, or someone who's never caught a trout before, put a rod in their hands, and have them catch a fish. And when they do, when something down there grabs their hook and they realize that they're connected to a wild trout by a thin thread, the watching is a hundred times more fun than if you were doing the catching.

A few years back I watched Toady Watson catch his first trout in Milkshake Lake. It was a very fine fish by anyone's standard, a 16-inch rainbow, all silver and football-fat. The look of disbelief and surprise when it struck, then the fear when he recognized he might lose the fish, and finally the laughing, giggling joy and pride that came aboard with that trout were worth a thousand trout of my own. Nothing existed for him but that fish. I have never seen such intense concentration, or elation, as when the trout was his. He will remember that moment all his life, and so will I.

That kind of wonder isn't limited to kids, either. Last year I showed the wife of a retired doctor how to catch her first trout, fishing a big nightcrawler over a submerged cutbank. When the fish picked up the worm and began to gnaw, she chanted over and over in a soft, wondrous whisper "Isn't that marvelous . . . isn't that simply marvelous?" And it was. Those fish were trophies to all of us, and they'll hang on the walls of my mind forever.

Have you been noticing the carry of this little boat? I've barely put my back into these oars, and we're at the upper end of the lake already. No hits at all? Perhaps they would have taken a spinning lure. Their glitter, flash, and erratic path will sometimes take trout when they refuse other things, but they're back in the car. See why I like that little Leonard? Flexibility. It seems that whenever I'm flyfishing, at least once a day I'd like to have a lure. Or vice versa. Someday I'm going to figure out a proper place to put that broomstick.

This place is worth a try, though. If they're biting at all, they'll be biting here. See the inlet stream up among those willows and bog? It will wash any food it is carrying down toward us, and trout will bank up in these gentle currents swirling out into the lake. Let me position the boat a little better so you can cast

across-current. When water is barely moving, that's the best way
to present a sunk fly of any kind, because the flow helps keep
slack out of your line and you can feel the strike immediately.

Don't spool that extra line back onto the reel . . . you need all
the reach you can get. Perhaps it's because the fish can see the
fisherman through the smooth pane, or they like to follow for
long distances in still water . . . I can't say for sure. But I'll
guarantee that the person who casts the farthest will catch the
most fish in a lake, and that is as true of spinning as of flycasting.
Mending line is a different proposition, too. In lakes you do have
to give a nymph some action, so along with experimenting with
patterns, you have to play with retrieve styles.

The standard is the same one you have been using all along,
except that as you reach for the line and begin your draw, give it
a series of tugs as you bring the line in, so that the fly jerks
underwater. Mend slowly at first, at a rate of around a foot every
5 seconds. Slow mends sometimes are easier when you use the
hand-twist retrieve . . . take in enough line to span your palm,
and roll it over your index finger. Slip your finger free and move
the doubled line to your palm. Roll the line over your pinky, slip
it into your palm, and roll it over your index finger again. The
hand-twist retrieve is advantageous because it's easy to engineer
little jerks into a very slow-moving fly, but it also creates shooting problems when you're handling 50 feet or more of line. The
coils tend to foul each other in your hand. Whatever style feels
most comfortable, if the trout turn down a very slow retrieve,
gradually step up the rate to five or six feet every 5 seconds.

Say . . . things are a little different than they were back at the
bridge. That last cast must have reached out 60 feet! But before
you get too smug, do you see how you've had a little help? For
one thing, you're higher in relation to the surface of the water
than if you were wading in a stream. That means you can drop
your backcast a few feet farther without it slapping the water
and dragging against your forward cast. The other advantage is
the line you are coiling at your feet. When you make your

shooting cast, there is no friction with the water or the palm of your hand as it reaches out there. Simple, isn't it? Simple and pleasant. Like I said, I can really get into lakes.

You'll find that sink-tip line is in order about 85 percent of the time on a lake, too. When there's no surface activity, trout will suspend at 5- to 10-foot depths, seldom deeper than that, and that's the same level that a sinking tip rides at.

If the fish were nymphing on top, or taking dries, you'd have to switch arbors to the weight-forward floating line for maximum reach, but size-up lake rises very carefully. They'll appear to be taking flies off the top. There might even be a bunch of adult flies on the water, but the majority of the rises in a lake will always be nymphing rises.

They can be awfully deceptive, too. A tiny dimple can have a 4- or 5-pound trout under it. Gulpers are what I call them, and they inhabit every lake I've fished. I learned how to catch them by accident, messing around in the fall on bluebird days when the ducks weren't flying. They always hang out around the same weedy flats that the ducks like, and I'd see them dimpling, but everyone told me they were chubs and suckers. Then one day I took a fly rod when I went hunting . . . casting practice again . . . and tossed a Gold-ribbed Hare's Ear in the middle of one of those dimples. There was no holding that fish. My leader was too light, and I wasn't ready for such power. He got down into the duck-weed and broke me off, just that quick. But that was the crack in the door, and by building on that one experience, I finally got it open. Great sport, and very unusual. You've got to use long leaders and backbreaking casts, and fish over the flats. You row or canoe up to the rises very quietly; an outboard puts the fish down. But if you do it right, and hit them right on the head with a Hare's Ear or a Wooly Worm or a Hodges, you can take a 2- to 5-pound trout about every other cast. You have to stalk those fish just like a deer. It's a lot like bonefishing.

One other thing you'll learn about them is that the way you retrieve your line counts. There's no set pattern. Some days they want a Wooly Worm deep and slow, and other days they won't look at a fly unless it's very small, and fished fast, just under the surface film so that it creates a little wake. You have to experiment with the retrieve, but once you hit on the right one, and are in tune with the fish, they'll strike all day, even at high noon in the summer when the sun is like a hammer.

They can be caught on spinning gear too, but the technique is different and you won't catch as many. You have to sneak up to good casting range, and drop a spoon beyond the rise by 20 feet. Then you crank as fast as you can, so that the lure is really cutting a wake. I've seen brown trout big as logs chase down a Dardevle, open their cotton-white mouths, and engulf that lure like an alligator swallowing a duck.

Damn, I wish I had a spinning rod right now! Don't ask me why I didn't bring it in the first place. I could have followed up right behind you on the stream, and the way things have gone, I'd probably have caught a lot more fish than you. When there's no encouragement or evidence that the fish are after bugs, a wise man turns to jewelry.

Now why are you laying your rod up? Keep trolling as I row back. Change the fly if you want, but keep trolling. There are a lot of pregnant postulates in troutfishing, but there is one rule that is ironclad and infallible: You can't catch a trout unless your line is in the water. It's the same with hunting. Last year the conditions were terrible in deer camp; the woods were as dry as boxed breakfast cereal and about as crunchy. Everyone was complaining about it and hanging around camp. You can't hunt from behind the walls of a log cabin; you've got to be in the woods to be hunting, and that's where I went. Got a pretty nice buck on the last day too, the only deer that came through camp. So just keep your line in the water and you might be pleasantly surprised. You're not going to find them striking at a fly through the floorboards of this old boat.

When we get back to shore, I'd guess we should work back toward the car and get spinning gear. It looks like flies aren't going to do the trick today. You could whip the water the rest of the afternoon, and maybe take a trout or two, but it wouldn't complement the conditions that exist; just be the sign of a zealot.

But there's one more approach to try with flies. You've been working them upstream all along, why not work them downstream on the way back?

No, it's not really a contradiction. I still believe that casting into the current creates the most natural impression, but fishing with the flow creates a wholly different effect. The current and its drag on your line carry your fly in a long, looping swing. It isn't exactly natural, but it can be provocative, especially when trout are proving obstinate. Second, downstream fishing covers more water, more quickly than upstream fishing. It's possible that you either neglected or misread some likely stations while working upstream. The nature of this approach puts the probability that you'll cover everything on your side. Finally, downstream fishing is fast, easy fishing. You seldom need more than a simple rollcast to place your fly, the line is always taut so you feel every take, and about half the fish hook themselves. You are also wading with the current, which moves you right along, and each presentation takes about 10 seconds to complete. Downriver fishing is a kind of last resort, a last-chance-for-everybody-to-take-my-fly technique, that not only catches fish, but fits very nicely into the patterns of working a stream.

When you are working with the current, stick with the sink-tip. The push of the current elevates the fly too far above feeding zones with floating line. I'm also a strong believer in using a dropper rig—a streamer or bucktail on the leader end, with a nymph or wet fly on a second 6-inch leader, tied with a blood knot a foot ahead of the streamer. Just knot some extra leader to the end of your tippet, and let 6 inches of the working end extend beyond the completed knot. The arrangement works a bit of nature into your retreive; a minnow will swim cross-current and upcurrent. And if something is suckered in by the odd behavior of the fly in front of it, don't try to explain why, but rejoice in the mistake.

There are two ways you can work a fly with the current. Your best shot is to wade down the middle of the river and cast to either bank. Make your throw at a 45 degree angle to the shore, and allow the current to bow and seize the line. As the loop swings out and down, work the fly in short jerks. You needn't strip line in; just hold it in your mending hand and twitch away. When the line is directly downstream from you, cast to the opposite bank. When that presentation is complete, move downstream and cast again.

We both saw some parts of Back Brook where wading down the middle was an impossibility, though. Casting from the bank is the only alternative, but it is second best. Get to the side of the stream opposite your casting arm, and make every effort to reach the far bank with your fly. For some unaccountable reason, flies fished in this way seem most appealing to trout stacked against banks.

Working downstream will be appealing to you in another way, as hard as you've been fishing in the stream. It's relaxing sport . . . almost lazy when set alongside dry-flies and nymphs fished on a dead drift. You glide along with the current, lobbing long, looping rollcasts to either bank, and you have more of a chance to take the whole stream in. Fishing upstream is singular and brilliant in its intensity; after a while you get a headache from the concentration. Downstream fishing is mindless, good-natured, and a springhead of daydreams . . . a great way to go when the trout aren't biting, because after a while, you really won't care if they are or not.

Help me tug that boat back up in these weeds, and then go on ahead. I'll hang behind and poke around. I've been talking an awful lot, and solitude will be a nice companion for you for a change. I want to look for mushrooms, and stream watch, and maybe look for patterns in the clouds from a bed in the meadow.

It's turning into one of those blue-and-puffy days that are made for a little siesta.

I'll meet you by those rapids below the falls. We haven't fished there yet, and that was spinning water if I ever saw it. Perhaps by the time we meet again, I'll have thought up some new ideas. If you're going to be serious about catching a trout, you've got to be creative as well as optimistic. And would you bring the paper bag? I don't know about you, but I'm getting hungry.

9 / *Bring Them Silver and Gold*

You're back sooner than I expected. I'd guess that fishing downstream wasn't all that productive. When the trout are biting, you tend to arrive late for meetings and forget things you were supposed to bring. I see you remembered my lunch.

That was some otter-slide of a trail coming down into here from above. Funny thing about steep climbs. You think they're tough going up because you puff so much, but they're really harder on the muscles in your legs when you're coming down. You have to brake the weight of your body with each step when you're descending, and it really puts the pressure on calves and thighs.

I've watched the river go by for 10 minutes and haven't seen a bit of activity . . . on the water at least. The sky is a different matter. Have you noticed how those cumulus clouds are building in the West? Creamy and billowy on top, but dark and sullen on the bottom. As hot and humid as the day has become, I wouldn't be surprised if we had a thunderstorm later on. As always, I left my raingear hanging in the garage. If I would just remember to bring it, I'd never be troubled with rain. It never rains when you bring a raincoat. At least it's not too far to the station wagon from here if the weather really gets threatening.

Want some? It's smoked trout with cream-cheese on black bread. It has a finer flavor than the most expensive imported salmon. At home I like to wash it down with icy-cold rosé . . . just a sip. You're supposed to drink rosé just chilled, but I prefer it as cold as I can get it. I put it in the freezer, and frost the wine glass before I serve it. You get a wonderfully clean, tart taste when it's that cold.

Try some of this, too. It's deer jerky. Absolutely marvelous stuff when you're troutfishing and want a bite to eat. Just put it in your mouth and chew until it's soft. One strip of jerky and a drink of springwater will fill you up for hours. Here, take some more and carry it in your pocket. It can't spoil.

We can take some comfort in that we're scoring on a par with Mother Nature. I've been watching that osprey fish, and he did as well as we; one caught and one missed. In a way, though, you've done even better than that bird; you've made new discoveries, learned new ways to fish, and you know that the trout aren't onto flies today. That's something gained.

And there have been those moments when your vision tunneled, and you were inside a circle, so it hasn't really been a bad day up to now, just not quite as good as it can be. We took a calculated risk. We both agreed that Back Brook looked a little better for lures than for flies, but even if conditions had clearly indicated flies were in order, and we had caught no fish, I would want to take a few casts with a lure. Trout have a habit of not abiding by all the rules we set up for them.

Take a day last fall on the Roaring River. An old friend had flown in from out of state to fish with me, and we'd been cabin-

bound for three days by an equinoctial storm. The rain changed to snow, and by the time it ended, there were 3 inches of wet, white slush along the riverbank.

I would never have gone fishing if he hadn't been there. Snow always shuts everything down, even baitfishing. But when we got to Pop's Pool, the place was carpeted with a hatch of # 16 Blue Duns, and boiling with trout. If you spread your fingers out over the water, your hand would cover five or six flies. Fish were coming up for them everywhere, and between the two of us, we took 31 rainbows and browns on dry-flies that afternoon. The only thing you really know about troutfishing is that you never know what is going to happen, and that persistent question leads you to the water's edge as much as the fish you hope to catch.

So press that 6-pound spool into place, thread the guides, and let's see what happens. There's still a lot of ground we haven't covered, and lures have an appeal all their own.

You can't really compare lure fishing to fishing streamers or bucktails, either. A fly rod evolved as the most practical means to fish flies, not big minnow imitations, Bucktails and streamers are a relatively recent development in the history of flyfishing, an adaption that afforded a means for a guy with a fly rod to imitate minnows when trout turned down insects. But like any compromise, the end product is less than ideal. With a fly rod, you can't take in line by hand with as much speed, and with as much nervous activity, as a real baitfish would exhibit. There's also the matter of buoyancy. Real minnows hug bottom, and unless you're using a heavily weighted fly . . . another medium fly rods cannot handle well . . . streamers and bucktails ride close to the surface, even with high-density sinking line.

A fly rod just can't fish a minnow imitation properly, to its maximum effect, and that's why I rarely put the two together. It's not the only mismatch in troutfishing, either. I feel the same way about spinning with an insect imitation. Bubble floats and spin-a-fly lines can never match the performance of a fly rod at this job. They are just as awkward, out of place, and unnatural as trying to handle a big, weighted streamer with a fishing system intended to cast a feather.

May I have that lure box for a second? You seem confused about a choice, and it's understandable. When you consider the possible combinations of weights, shapes, styles, and colors, you end up with more silver and gold than is in the United States Treasury. But actually, matching the most logical lure to stream conditions is a more predictable exercise than picking artificial flies. Baitfish don't exhibit the enormous variety that you find in the insect world. So it's easier to evaluate lures with a set of principles that lead to a firm conclusion.

You can sort them out into four classes, and each class is defined as much by the place you're going to cast the lure as the trout you're after.

I do use streamers and bucktails, but I use them on the end of a spinning rod, with a heavy split shot, 6 inches ahead of the fly, as a casting weight. They're often the best way to fish a lake or the slowest water in a stream because of their unusual action. You have to jerk them and bob them if they're going to be appealing, but the one quality they possess that other lures don't is near-neutral buoyancy. They won't flutter or fall to the bottom the instant forward motion ceases. If you are jigging them, the lead shot ahead of the hook bounces with each jerk. It rises, reaches an apex, and then begins to fall. As it does, the streamer remains virtually motionless, with the exception of its feather or bucktail dressing, which recovers and fans out like the puff of a parachute. Jerk again, the fly shoots forward, the shot bounces upward, and the effect is repeated. No other lure has this appearance, not even a weighted streamer or a jig, and it can be very appealing to trout. Another place where I like to fish a streamer with spinning gear is over the lip of a riffle. Jig it across the bottom of the hole just below a broken bar, and if a trout is in a feeding mood, he's likely to pick it up.

Plugs will take trout when you fish them over still or slow-moving water. I don't know why, but they seem to produce best when you troll them in lakes. Another place where I like to use a plug is in big, rotating eddies and deep, slow pools. They are also superb producers should you be addicted to troutfishing after dark. In the daylight hours, they don't usually catch the most fish, but what they take will be of substantial size.

Spinners have universal appeal. They'll tempt a trout in a brook, stream, river, or lake, but you must match your lure to the water you're fishing. Although the principle of this lure is standard: a metal blade, steel shaft, and solid metal or plastic body, variations in the width and length of the blade and the size and weight of the body produce different characteristics of performance. For example, a quarter-ounce body, fitted with a broad, oval blade, will whirl much faster and run closer to the surface than the same body fitted with a narrow willow blade, assuming that the rate of retrieve is constant in both cases. The determining factor in performance is a complex relationship between the working surface of the moving blade, the total weight of the lure, and the rate of retrieve. Rather than going through an extensive explanation of physics, it's easier to hedge on a rule of thumb. Use wide blades with light bodies in still waters, and as the rate of streamflow increases, use narrower blades and heavier bodies.

The reasoning behind this rule is derived from the fact that trout are most likely to strike any lure when it is fished slow and deep, and these guidelines should put you in that range. Some of the lures that are best suited to still or slow-moving waters are this Mepps Aglia and the Panther Martin. Two of my favorites in swift water are the Aglia Long and the Doty Raider. A good example of a midrange spinner is this Swiss Swing.

Spinners are most attractive to trout when the water is milky. They produce a lot of flutter and flash at slow speeds, so they are easier to see . . . and catch up with . . . than other lures. I also fish spinners whenever trout seem reluctant to bite, and again, I think their appeal at such times is directly related to speed. Other classes of lures must be retrieved at a relatively fast pace. If trout are not on feed, they're not interested in a spirited chase,

it's just too much effort. But when an invitation to an easy meal drifts slowly by their nose in a burst of gaudy glitter, the opportunity is just too golden for some trout to ignore.

Spoons have a single metal blade that may assume a shape anywhere from that of a teaspoon to a gently-curving "S." They are my all-around choice for rivers and streams when the water runs from slightly discolored to crystal clear. Spoons are generally the fastest-moving of all trout lures, but fish have no trouble seeing and tracking them when the water is clear.

And track them they will, for this class of hardware packs a double-barreled appeal. At slow speeds, they weave side to side in graceful, alluring curves, tracking the same path in water as the ski technique known as "wedlin" tracks in snow. When the pressure of the water working against them increases, they spin along a narrow axis, their flattish bodies now creating an illusion of a fat baitfish in frantic flight. Realize that this change in the lure's attitude is bound to occur naturally, without any special effort on your part, as it enters and leaves conflicting pockets of current. The impression is that of a lazing minnow who suddenly spots danger and tries to get away. This two-stage action excites any fish that sees it, and it lies at the core of the spoons' extraordinary appeal.

Like spinners, spoons must be tuned to water conditions. The depth and speed at which they work is determined by the relationship between their total weight and the size of their working surface. Lighter, larger spoons respond at slower speeds, and run more shallow, than heavy, narrow spoons. When I'm fishing slow-moving water, I usually bait up with a light, stamped-metal spoon like this Thomas. In moderately fast water, I prefer heavy, wide, cast metal spoons like that Wonderlure or the Dardevle. In swift water, very thick, heavy lures like the Kamlooper, or narrow, snakelike spoons like the Krocodile brand perform best.

Just as you'll learn the types of lures that appeal to trout, you'll also find a lot that won't. Serious troutfishermen are usually innovators, who dream of someday stumbling upon a heretofore unknown technique that knocks 'em dead, and I'm of that camp. I have experimented with things like surface plugs, spinner baits, and plastic worms, often in the middle of feeding binges when I had no trouble taking fish on conventional hardware. Virtually every oddball bait I tried was unproductive. A few elicited a follow-up or two, but not a strike. It suggests that trout do not strike from curiosity or anger, but because they want something to eat, and that the most appealing lures will always resemble small fish, at least in the water.

See how I've also got them sorted by size rather than type? That's something to consider too. I have seen keeping-size trout strike at lures that were anywhere from one-third their size to the smallest bauble of jewelry that could be threaded on a line, but there is a better middle ground. Figure that trout are most likely to take a lure that is between one-tenth and one-twentieth their size, and fish the smaller end of this scale over water that is clear, heavily pressured, or both.

An implicit question arises at this point. If you use very large lures, will you catch only very large trout and bypass all the small fry? I've put that theory to the test too, and it has proven true. But another fact of trout life that was also affirmed was that there are very few really big fish in a stream, and that those that are there aren't always hungry. Fishing with big lures is as slow as a turtle race. It makes far more sense to use modest-sized lures unless you're out to set a record.

There will also be times when it makes sense to use the tiniest lures in the box, even though you're casting over the kind of water that suggests big fish.

For some unaccountable reason, sophisticated trout will be far more interested in a thumbtack-sized lure than something big, even if the fish are large. That's why you should always pack those ultralite lures along. Even though you're using a standard weight spinning rod, you can still fish very light lures by clamping a piece of shot onto your line, just as when fishing streamers. There are other parallels between the appeal of ultralite lures and streamers, too. Because they are so light, tiny lures don't sink so fast, and they exhibit a few of the streamer's jigging qualities. That lightness also translates into a great deal of action at very slow speeds. And, since any type of ultralite lure can be worked much slower than a heavy lure, all of them have the same attraction as spinners. But they are different from other lures in one important respect . . . that heavy chunk of lead. It carries those tiny lures deep, down to where the fish are. Quite often a trout will take a tiny lure and shot combination when it won't look at anything else. It's an important trick to remember.

Color is the final factor when you're looking for a lure with a lot of appeal, and in most cases, you should base your selection on the color of the water you're fishing.

Going back to the observation that trout are most prone to strike at lures that resemble familiar foods, realize that all fish are a little like chameleons. They have the ability to change their color to match their background, thereby gaining protective camouflage.

For example, trout taken from a stream with a bright, sandy bottom will appear silvery, with washed-out colors. Those taken from a stream paved with dark boulders will be dark with rich, prominent markings.

The same thing happens in response to water clarity. A very clear lake tends to yield silvery fish. Cloudy or muddy water enriches coloration.

Baitfish, as well as trout, have a similar response to their environment, so that evaluating the color . . . or clarity . . . of the water you're fishing will tell you what color lure to use.

Realize, however, that all fish are made up of two contrasting shades. They have bright sides and bellies, and dull, dark backs. Proportionately, their side and stomach account for the most predominant hue, and this relationship should always be reflected in a trout lure.

I've found that the most productive trout hardware always has a substantial amount of shine, with an area that mirrors silver, gold, or copper accounting for one-third or more of the lure's surface. Many of my favorites run a ratio of two-thirds or more glitter to one-third or less of color, and at times, usually when the water's dirty, solid gold, silver, or copper will get the most strikes.

With these guidelines in mind then, think about the way water changes color during the course of a season. It goes from muddy, to cloudy or milky, to clear, right? Well, baitfish would adapt to that change; I've seen a captive trout go from dark to light overnight, so let the stream pick the color.

When the water is very clear, or the bottom of a stream is very bright, use a silver lure. When it's mildly discolored use gold, and when it's muddy, match the color of the silt load. Brown silt would dictate copper, light-colored silt silver.

There are corresponding accent colors to these shades, too. Did you ever notice how a trout caught from a very clear lake will appear to have a blue or green back? That's the kind of thing that determines accent colors. Blue, gray, or green generally go with silver, and black with copper and gold. Red goes with everything. No matter the color of the water, all fish have red gills. Colors that I've found don't particularly appeal to trout are browns and pastels. Yellow is a borderline case. Black-bladed spinners or bodies with yellow dots represent about the only productive use of yellow that I've found, probably because it appears golden when it's in the water and working.

And here's another odd one. Fluorescent orange is an excellent accent color to use when you fish in the West, but I've never had any luck with it in the East. I can't come up with any explanations for that one, but it's a good thing to remember.

Now with Back Brook to guide you, make an educated guess about an appropriate lure.... Fine ... a 3/8-ounce Thomas Cyclone, with red dots. A logical choice, but for one thing. This is swift water down here; the current probably averages five knots and the river is deep. The lure is too thin and broad for its weight to get down to where the fish are. Try again ...

. . . You know how to use tackle well, and how to match a trout's mood. Adding that cannonball shot to the Cyclone should pull it right to the bottom, and the size of the lure and the action you'll get just might turn these fish on. One other addition I'd recommend is a snapswivel. Lures larger than a quarter-ounce put up enough water resistance to twist monofilament line into unmanageable kinks, especially in fast water, unless you use a swivel!

Adding a tiny snapswivel won't detract from that lure's overall appearance or action, either. I do think this happens when you're fishing ultralite lures, though. Lures a quarter-ounce or smaller become elongated with a snapswivel. The swivel becomes part of the fish illusion, so I don't use it with ultralite lures. Swivels aren't really necessary in that case, anyway. Tiny lures don't twist line so badly. Another place not to use a swivel is with a plug or streamer. Neither of them will twist a line, so why chance an unnatural impression?

Listen . . . Was that thunder? I thought I heard some rumbling, but it's hard to distinguish from the roar of the river. The sky looks clear enough, although we're not seeing that much of it from down here. Thunderstorms come up fast at this time of the year; we were lucky to leave the lake when we did.

But we'd better get back to fishing. Try a few casts right here. Water that moves at these velocities is way too swift for a fly, and very difficult to cover with bait, but people try it anyway. They never get down deep enough, down where the fish are, which is the same as not fishing the water at all. Practically speaking, fast water . . . lure water . . . tends to be the most underfished in any stream, and even the average lure fisherman works it wrong, just as you're doing now.

Across-current and downcurrent casts hold the least potential in fast water. When you make your retrieve, no matter how slowly you take in line, the effect of the moving water against the lure elevates it way above the slow zones on the bottom. The right way to fish a lure is the same way you fished a fly; cast it upriver into the current lanes that lead past probable stations.

You'll also get a lot more distance out of your cast if you learn to use the backbone of the rod to help propel your lure. Face your target, bring the shaft back to the One O'clock position, and snap the lure forward, like cracking a whip. That puts the fast tip to work behind the lure along with the acceleration of your forward cast. Before, you were getting most of your carry out of the forward sweep of the shaft alone. That's called a soft cast. There's a place for it, but not when you're using a lure. In order to make the most of a fast-tip action, to enjoy the design of the shaft and the performance it can deliver, you've got to snap your lure out there. It's like the difference between throwing a rock and shooting one out there with a slingshot.

That's it . . . could you feel it? And look at how much more distance you got. A good 20 feet. It's the same principle as flycasting. You've got to load the rod if you're going to make the most out of a cast.

You've discovered something else, too: that parallel casting up current lanes in swift, wide streams can only be done over a quarter of the water. In order to reach the rest of it, you would have to wade, and that's impossible here.

There's one other cast to learn that will cover the rest of the water, that's called the turnaround. I hit on it a few years ago. Like most spinfishermen, I used to work a lure in the same patterns everywhere; standing in a spot along a stream bank or lakeshore, casting to the clock, Nine to Three. It's a good pattern for a lake, or in slow, flat water, but in places like this, I began to realize that there was one cast that was taking every fish I caught. Even more remarkably, there was one moment during the retrieve that seemed magic in its attraction for trout. Although it represented only 5 percent of the time my lure was in the water, it accounted for 40 percent of my strikes.

The numbers were different but the cast was always the same; when the river ran left to right, a Ten O'clock cast was charmed. When it ran right to left, the Two O'clock cast took fish. It was a real puzzle, but one that I became determined to solve. When the pieces finally fit together, they revealed a spinning technique of enormous appeal that's ideally suited to water that's difficult to fish.

Trout are commonly portrayed as shy, reclusive creatures. Nothing could be further from the truth.

Trout are shy, but shy like a stalking lioness, skulking in the shadows until her prey comes within range. Reclusive? Only when they suspect that they're in danger of becoming a meal for something else. Dainty? Not in terms of their eating habits. They will fill themselves to a point where minnows half their size gorge their gullet, and still strike a lure. For all the romantic prose written about them, a trout is no less a predator than a wolf, eagle, or barracuda. If they grew as large as sharks, you can bet that wading wouldn't be nearly so popular as it is today.

Just as fox, coyote, and bobcat are drawn to the chilling cries of a rabbit in distress, predatory fish will zero in on any extraordinary behavior exhibited by their prey.

A big brown will ignore a school of baitfish swimming by, until one member of the school starts swimming in odd, jerky circles. Then he'll rocket in and have it in a blink. A lone minnow can swim to within two feet of a finning rainbow, and he'll pay the minnow no heed. But frighten the minnow so he turns and scoots, and the trout will be on him like a cat. Make no mistake, trout, especially large trout, are hardly good guys by human standards. Their first choice in prey is always the crippled, the slow, the weak, or the fearful, and therein lies the appeal of this cast. It creates the illusion of a frantic, frightened baitfish, trying desperately to get away, because he has come face-to-face with his maker. To do it, you have to be able to maneuver your lure through a three-stage change in behavior, right in front of a likely station in the stream.

The first stage is action. In an instant, a lure that's been lazing along at a leisurely wobble starts fluttering wildly. The suggestion is that an injured baitfish has recognized imminent danger, and is now in wild flight.

The second stage is an 180 degree turnaround in a horizontal direction; coincidental with the switch in appearance, the lure reverses its path and heads the other way.

The third stage is in a vertical direction. As the lure swings around, it also rises sharply off the bottom, providing the trout with an easy target that's silhouetted against the surface. This illusion of fear, the shift into evasive tactics, and the appearance of a clear target combine to trigger the predatory urge in trout so surely that they can't resist the itch to strike out and snare another morsel, just because it's trying to get away. It's the same thing that trout fall for when you're trolling and you make a turn.

If you want to learn how to create this effect, we'd better find a spot with fewer hydraulics. Straight, fast, but otherwise flat water is the kind of place in which you should practice. I know a perfect spot on the other side of this rockslide; a swift run.

Be careful going up and over. There are an awful lot of imagined dangers in the outdoors, but you're tottering over a very real one. Rocks the size of an executive desk can be balanced so precariously that the press of a hand will tip them. And while we're up here, take a look way upstream and then down below us. See the pattern again? Smooth water, whitewater, smooth water . . . a stream unit. It is swifter and straighter and more violent than you've seen before, but the same laws apply.

Watch it very carefully as you're going down. That's the time when things are most likely to slide because your weight hits the rocks all at once.

There it is again . . . No doubt this time; thunder. This might have to be a very quick lesson.

To make the cast, you've got to face upstream, and envision the shoreline as Nine and Three on the clock. Make your cast to Two O'clock, and snap your bail shut the instant the lure hits the water. Start reeling.

Take in line just fast enough to keep the slack out as the current gets behind the lure and pushes it along. Keep your eye on the slack; the current speed will probably vary, and you want to reel just slightly faster than it's moving. This makes for a lure that's slowly rotating or wobbling, and sinking as it heads downriver.

This part of the retrieve is the trickiest in some respects, because you want the lure to skim bottom, but not hang up. If you feel the tick of streambed rock, reel a little faster. If the lure blasts up to the surface as it turns around, you're reeling too fast.

When you're retrieving at the correct speed, your line will have developed a deep belly as the lure reaches a point opposite us. Depending on the swiftness of the current, stop taking in line a few seconds either side of this moment. The water will catch the belly, and the pressure on the line will keep the lure moving on its own.

A few seconds later, the lure will begin to accelerate, due to whiplash. The bellied line, your stationary rod and reel, and current drag combine to move the line faster and faster as it approaches the lure. You can identify this acceleration because you'll feel a pronounced increase in the pressure the line is exerting on your rod tip as your lure begins to work faster and faster, setting up progressively greater resistance. At this point, lift your rod tip high enough so the line clears the water. The current still has a firm grab on the lure at this point, and it takes all the slack out of the line. When the line draws up tight, the lure reverses direction and starts to angle toward the surface.

The time for a turnaround lasts between 7 and 12 seconds. In a strong current you need not touch your reel, just be ready for a strike, which brings up another dictum; don't snap your rod so high that you'll be handicapped when you strike to set the hook. In a slower current, you might have to take in line as the lure goes around and up. Again, the key is in the pressure you feel on your rod tip. It should remain constant from the point of whiplash until the retrieve is complete.

After the turnaround is made and the lure has risen, you will feel a decrease in rod tip pressure. Water and whiplash effect have done their job and the only thing working against the lure now is the current. Pace your retrieve so that the lure continues to flash and flutter as it comes into shore. Although trout are most likely to strike at the point of turnaround, this occasionally just piques their interest. When this happens, they'll follow for a while, and strike later. Make it a practice to jig your lure two or three times as it's coming to you, so that it looks like it's trying to "escape" again. That extra little enticement has caught me a lot of fish that ordinarily would have lost interest, and it can do the same for you.

Now that you've got the technique down, let's find some richer water to mine. The same essential skills apply here that applied earlier. First you identify stations, then you assess flow lines. Your cast must be accurate . . . to a spot where the combined vectors of your retrieve and the direction of the river lead the lure so that the moment of turnaround occurs within sight of a probable trout. The water around that rockslide looks good to me. A rotating eddy spun off the foot of it, and some hellishly big boulders must have come bouncing down at one time to make those midstream hydraulics.

I'd try the rotating eddy first, it's the closest and the easiest to fish. I'd recommend you stand right opposite the tail of the eddy fence. Cast upriver 45 degrees, and direct the turnaround so that it occurs just as the lure crosses the fence. Reel a little faster, raise your rod tip . . . now!

Good execution on the turnaround, but you cast a little bit too far. The current pushed the lure too far downriver, and it turned around beyond the fence. You've got good lateral control when you cast, but your distance accuracy needs practice. Next time, get your eye on the lure and your target at the same time. Look at the *whole* picture, and feather the line so the lure drops down on target. I get the best results by encircling the moving line between my thumb and forefinger halfway between the reel and the butt guide. The tighter the circle, the more feathering effect you'll get.

Perfect! You've caught a vector that should have you turning around right on the fence. Up with the rod tip . . . you've got it!

Now all you have to do is step upriver another six feet, and repeat the pattern. You want to present a series of turnarounds that trace the eddy fence, or any place where a trout is likely to be lying in wait. Just keep working up into it until you feel that you've made a presentation to every potential fish along the fence, and don't forget the eddy apex. That's a little tricky, too. In order to cover it, you usually have to stand right on the point that is making the eddy. The turnaround occurs within a few feet of your rod tip, but it still charms trout.

I was once showing Jay Feldman how to do a turnaround, at a big rotating eddy just like this. Except that Jay had trouble envisioning what I meant. So I took the rod and made a cast, explaining just what was happening as the lure was drifting down. When I reached the turnaround point, right at the apex of a rotating eddy, I said, "the trout should strike right . . . about . . . now." At that instant, a 6½-pound brown grabbed the lure and tore off downstream. No one was more astonished than I, but I handled it all very matter-of-factly. Somehow I got the fish into a too-small net, at which point I handed Jay his rod and said, "There, I've shown you once and don't ask me to do it again." Every time we see each other, and it isn't often enough, one of us will tell that story.

Nothing. . . . Not even on the apex. Try plugging away at that midstream sleeper. You're doing everything correctly. All that's left is to read your water and fish to stations.

There goes the sun, and it's getting dark as soot in the west. Notice how the flies are getting to be annoying; and the way the leaves on the willows are showing their undersides. They're two more signs of rain on the way. As black as it is beyond the canyon mouth, I would say there's a squall line about to pass over, then much cooler weather. A big change.

The fishing? I don't know. I've never been able to predict that fishing will get worse or better by changes in the weather, but I have seen fish behavior change . . . trout that suddenly started to feed on top, or cut a feeding spree short, or that suddenly and inexplicably went wild over a lure that hadn't caught a thing all day. That's something else about fishing. You can go about it all very methodically, but there are so many variables that hunches are often as helpful as logic. So I'm going to play my hunches. After you cover the rest of this water, we'll work our way downstream, fishing as we go. We're going to get some rain out of this, and that could very well alter the complexion of things.

This has been a puzzling day in a lot of ways. To tell you the truth, I know Back Brook a little better than I've been letting on, and this is the slowest fishing I've ever seen here. I will tell you this with conviction, though. The trout are there, they have been finning in every place we've fished. They're just not on feed.

I have heard someplace that a trout empties his stomach through normal digestion every six hours. It doesn't convince me that trout get hungry in the same sense that we recognize hunger, but there is something to that six hour period. I've found that on slow days, if you have the time and inclination to stick with it, things eventually break loose.

There's one thing I am sure of, and it's that Back Brook isn't fished out. There aren't that many people who fish here, and even if there were, pressure is the least likely explanation for trout that seem to be in short supply. It's far more likely that you're either hamstrung by convention or conviction, or that you're not fishing to the trout that are there.

I used to think places could be fished out myself, until I watched the Fish and Game Department shock a stretch of the Roaring River. What an education that was!

Are you familiar with how electro-shocking works? Well, a direct electric current is pumped through a probe. When it hits a fish, he orients his head toward the current source, and sympathetic muscular response propels him forward. As soon as he comes to the surface, he's netted, weighed, measured and counted, and then he's returned to the stream.

The place the Department shocked was along the most popular part of the river, a stretch where there's family car access from either side. Because of the number of people who fish there, local legend has it that the place is fit only for tourists. That it's been fished out.

The first thing that impressed me was the number of trout the river gave up. The effect of the generator covered only about a 40-foot-wide swath, but after the first 300 yards they had to pull ashore and make a count because the holding tanks were full. They had 42 fish.

A mile below the start of the survey there was an old wagon ford, a broad, grassy flat in an otherwise narrow, swift channel. It's the most popular spot to fish in the whole river, and it also proved to have the densest population of trout!

Scratch the myth about places being fished out because they are heavily fished.

Another pattern I noticed was the location of the fish. Although the river was nearly 100 yards wide at this point, the greatest concentration of trout lay within four feet of the banks. As a matter of fact, the largest one that came up, a 4½-pound brown, was stationed behind a rock that was anchored to the bank 10 yards away from a heavily-used campsite. As you might expect, flat, featureless water turned up the least fish, and the smallest fish, too. It was obvious that trout like to congregate around hydraulics. When they were shocked up from the middle of the river, that's where they'd be.

Another possibility is that the fish are here, but that they're just smarter than we are. One of the myths that day did substantiate was that old fish tend to be wise fish. The same spot had been shocked earlier, and each fish recorded and tagged. The previously-tagged fish that were recovered were all of substantial size, about 1½-pounds and up. Records showed that quite a few smaller fish that had been tagged previously were no longer part of the population, they had been caught.

The returns of tags by fishermen also pointed to this conclusion: big fish are invariably smarter and more difficult to catch than their 10- to 12-inch kindred. For further proof, I submit Big Bertha.

On another shocking trip, to another river, I watched a 15-pound female brown roll up from under a cut bank. It was a smallish stream, 25 feet wide on the average, and nowhere near as popular as the Roaring River, but still, it is well known and fished hard by local anglers. Bertha resided not 100 yards from a paved highway, in a spot that was a favorite for worm fishermen. I use the past tense because she is no longer there. No, no one caught her. A fish of that size would have been celebrated over the surrounding five counties. The last time she was shocked up, two years ago, her condition was deteriorating, and they figured she eventually died of old age.

Your actions speak for themselves. Dawdling a lure in the water off your rod tip is a sure sign of a bored fisherman. If you'd rather, we'll head for the bridge right now. We're going to be rained out very shortly anyway; the birds have quieted down, and the flies aren't nearly so annoying. But I meant what I said about sticking with it. Things take odd little turns when you refuse to give up.

The lightning's getting close enough to be dangerous, too . . . wait, I'm counting.

. . . 29, 30. About 30 seconds between the flash and the thunder. The squall line is around six miles away, and they can move awfully fast. Better forget the fish for now and get back to the car. I don't particularly want to be under those big cotton-woods down in the valley with lightning popping and crackling right over our heads.

10 / *Hook, Line, and Sinker*

It's not rain, that's hail bouncing off the hood! There's one stroke of good luck we've had today; that we're not out in it. If you'd quit fishing one minute later, we'd have all that bouncing off us, and when they're the size of a marble, they raise a welt.

Interesting thing, that quality we call luck. You can look at it from so many perspectives. I used to take an elderly gent named Mulligan fishing now and then. He was a devout Catholic, and for a Christmas present, he once gave me a Saint Christopher medallion. The day after I pinned it to my sun visor, I had an accident . . . just a fender-bender. . . . but I pointed out the irony of it to Mulligan. You know what he said? "If it hadn't been there the accident would have been worse."

So in a way, it was lucky that we didn't start taking fish. We'd probably just be leaving now, and there's going to be some real fireworks out of this storm. Did you notice how the car windows steamed up the second you slammed the door? It means there's a radical change in barometric pressure and temperature going on ... the passage of a strong weather front ... and look at how gloomy it is here under the trees. Dark as dusk, and deep inside the bushes it's like night, except for the pale green glow of the young maples. As if they were charged with electricity, too.

It's eerie how everything shuts down; the calm before the storm. The flies, the birds, everything shelters under the thickest cover it can find. Even the air seems charged, not just by the storm, but by everything that's crouched and poised and hidden.

Wow! That was the closest bolt yet. When you hear that tearing sound, like a jet passing just overhead, they're right on top of you. I wonder if that could be the air being split by the lightning? It's a different sound than distant thunder. Thunder explodes and rolls, but when a lightning bolt hits very close it sounds like the heavens are being ripped apart.

The leading edge of the storm must be directly overhead. Here comes the rain. Droplets the size of a dime. Look at them hiss off the hood and churn up the road. It's coming down so hard that the drops are vaporizing on contact and making a close-hugging ground fog. This is more than just another thunderstorm, it's a real frog strangler!

Back Brook is in for some kind of change, and I would expect that it's going to be one for the better. Fishing couldn't get much worse. Do you know what phase the moon is in? I forget to check on that with the same regularity that I forget to bring my raingear.

I can tell you this; troutfishing is usually slow during a full moon, perhaps because the fish feed at night, or perhaps there is some other force at work. The phases of the moon are very important to salt water fishing, though. Fish always seem to bite best on the first and last quarter, and least on the dark and the full. It's easy to keep track of there, because the tidal charts I use also list moon phases in the boxes around the dates.

I wonder if I could figure out tides on a trout stream? Even though there would be no rise or fall, the pull of the moon is still there, and it might affect trout behavior in some predictable way. Tides change about every six hours, too. The six hour thing again. Patterns . . . catching trout has a lot to do with recognizing them.

For a moment there it looked like the storm was letting up, but here it comes again. The wind driving the rain in sheets, like waves on the sea. The rainsheets almost have the same rhythm as waves; pulsing, cresting, and then moving on. The only time you'll ever see it rain harder than this is during a hurricane.

Karma is another possibility. I don't know if I believe it either; I'm cursed with an objective nature. But I always remember a quote from *Hamlet:* "There are more things in heaven and earth, Horatio, than are dreamt of in your philosophy," and it goads me to at least consider odd explanations. There do seem to be certain days when too many things go wrong, or you feel you're not in tune with fishing. How do you explain that?

It's not my answer, but John Barsness once brought it up while we were sitting out a storm like this one. He thought he might have bad rod karma because he's always snapping off tips in car doors or stepping on guides, or breaking butt sections on a perfectly normal cast with no logical explanation for it . . . that sort of thing. And I've known people who fit the same description when it comes to catching trout. Joe Wigley for one.

We used to teach in the same university English department, and had offices across the hall. Joe would drop in to talk fishing between classes, and he kept insisting that he couldn't catch a trout no matter how hard he tried or who he fished with. That he was the angling equivalent of the Joe something-or-other in Al Capp's cartoon strip, who went around with a perpetual cloud over his head.

"The fish can be going wild," he once said, "and as soon as I show up, 'p-f-f-f-f-t,' the fireworks fizzle."

"Nonsense," I replied. "You're just doing something wrong," and I took him out several times to prove my point, but I

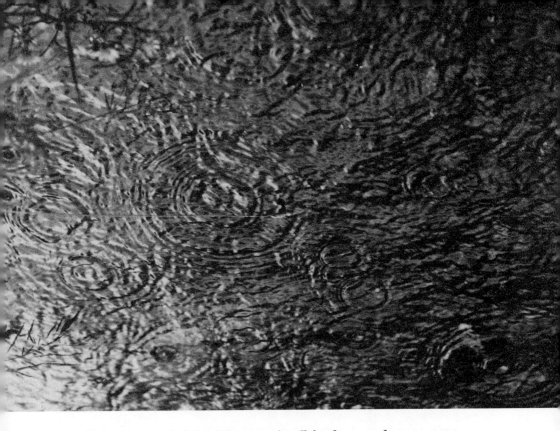

couldn't. Damned if the fish weren't off feed every day we went.

Then I ran into him up at Milkshake Lake. I'd been fishing the inlet channel from a boat, and had knocked 'em dead on flies; rainbows between 2 and 3 pounds. I saw him casting from the shore, not 200 yards away from where I'd been fishing.

"Quick Joe, hop aboard," I said, nosing toward him. "I'm going to prove something to you."

He climbed in, and we were back in the same spot where I'd caught the fish not 10 minutes earlier. I anchored us next to the same snag, and gave Joe my rod, with the same fly that had been so successful; a #14 wet Coachman. He dropped it right where I told him, give or take a foot or two. It was right in front of a submerged cutbank that lay in the middle of the inlet current.

He fished for 15 minutes, and didn't even have a strike. Then I tried, thinking perhaps that there was some subtle quirk in my presentation that was exciting the fish but that I wasn't perceiving.

I fished for half an hour and didn't get a strike.

Joe got awfully smug in an I-told-you-so way, and I don't think I ever fished with him after that; he moved to another state. But the story does have a happy ending.

I saw his daughter in an airport a few years later, and she said Joe was taking a lot of trout from the streams around his place, so bad trout karma, if there is such a thing, is either reversible or a function of geography.

And it could also be me, or some chemistry between the two of us. About once a year I get to fish with Ed Burlingame, another guy I don't see enough of, and we have never done well together. Usually when I take a friend to a very special place we always do well. Maybe not every time, but at least half the time.

I've taken Ed to the Gunflint, Lagoon Lake, Quicksilver Creek, the Roaring River . . . all my favorites . . . and our catch has been about as dismal as today. The strange thing is this; I know Ed to be a good and successful trout fisherman, and he knows me to be the same. We just can't seem to click with the trout when we fish together. How can you explain it?

The storm is passing. The time between the flash of lightning and the sound of thunder is stretching out, and it's getting brighter. The rain's let up too, but its effects will be around for a while. The road ditch looks like it's running a good 6 inches of water, and so will every trickle and rill that funnels into Back Brook. We must have had a good inch of moisture since it began.

Hear the robin? When they start to sing, the sun won't be too far behind. Let's get the bait rod set up, while we wait out the last of the rain. That storm could prove to be the best break we've had all day.

Don't forget to switch line spools as well as rods, and make sure you've got the can, the hooks and the weights somewhere in the vest. That's really all you'll need, but you might just as well pack the lures too. You've got the room, and it's always wise to keep your options open.

In some ways, baitfishing is the simplest way to catch a trout, the least absorbing. That is why most of us begin as baitfisher-men, but I like to end there. That's another nice thing about troutfishing, you can move either way through the circles.

But like anything else, baitfishing is really what you make of it. Take still fishing. That was Tom Sicard's love when he was alive; just bait up with a big worm, or a piece of sucker meat, and sit by the river and wait. Sounds simple, right? But I have never seen a still fisherman who was Tom's equal. He would always end up with more than anybody else with him, and he often caught more trout than I did, with all my careful planning. He knew something about the holes he fished, or how to rig a bait, or the trout he was after, better than anyone else, and I'm sure if I had taken the time to learn his thinking, I would have found still fishing just as much fun as he did. But I didn't. I was too wrapped up in flies and lures and drift fishing. Now he's gone and his knowledge with him, and you and I are the poorer for it.

Ah! The rain has stopped. Let's try our luck on Back Brook just once more. It should be easy to find a few worms, wet as every-thing is.

There's a lot more to be made of baitfishing than still fishing, though. When you really get into it, there are elements of the same pleasures you find in flyfishing and lure fishing. And I've found it to be the best way to catch really big trout. I've caught about 50 fish that I'd call trophies, 4 pound trout and larger, and of that number, better than three-quarters were taken on a natural bait. Flies will take the most trout, but when the condi-tions are right, bait always gets the big ones.

Let's try here. No, not fishing, picking bait. We've got to catch the bait before we can catch the trout, and that looks like a sure spot for a crawler or two, that hollow down next to the stream.

Just turn over rocks and rotted logs down where the earth is damp and ferny. They'll be underneath, waiting to come out of their holes as soon as darkness falls. There's a couple right here ... nightcrawlers the size of young snakes!

I don't know exactly why some people think baitfishing is

unsporting, or not at all enjoyable. I've hatched as many dreams picking worms like this as I have at my fly-tying table, and you'll find the skill needed to fish them well parallels some of the demands of fly and lure fishing. Probably just a misunderstanding of what's involved. But I will tell you this; baitfishing needs no apology.

How many? A dozen. That should be plenty, and if we run out, we can always find more. Bed them with grass, by the way. Loose earth will kill a worm. They suffocate in it.

We won't go as far as we did this morning, just to the canyon mouth. It's getting late, and I should think about going. I spent a lot more time with you than I had planned. No . . . I don't have to go yet. I still have a little time, and I'm having as much fun as you are.

See how Back Brook has changed color? It was milky to clear earlier and now it's definitely milky. My guess is that it will be dirty by dusk. Up there at the headwaters, trickle is joining trickle, rill is joining rill, and they're all dumping the results of the storm into Back Brook. It's on the rise, and it will probably peak early tomorrow morning. If you have the time, baitfishing should be supreme then. The rain will draw the crawlers out tonight and they'll be very active. Many will fall into the stream and, by morning, the trout will be zeroing in on them. You should be able to catch all you want.

Just as Royal Coachmen and green Wooly Worms are my favorite flies, worms are my favorite bait. Mainly because they're the easiest bait of all to catch, keep, and fish. That's another of worm fishing's unrecognized pleasures, a worm ranch. Catching and keeping your own bait is an exercise in integrity, like tying your own flies.

But worms won't work all the time. Trout respond to natural patterns, they don't order them. If worms aren't part of the natural scheme of the stream, they won't be the best bait. Although I find flies work better then, I have experimented with bait in late July and August when the ground was hot and dry and the worms down. Grasshoppers and crickets outfished worms three-to-one because they were in the natural pattern of things. For the same reason, minnows will outfish worms in the winter.

And in that vein, let me show you something about Back Brook. Do you see that dead backwater below the jam of logs? My bet would be that there isn't a trout in there right now, but if the creek rises a foot tonight—and it should—it will run higher than the dry flood channel above, and current will start to move through the backwater. The thalweg of the stream between here and there will carry more water and accelerate, and the trout will leave their stations in the middle of the stream and move into more comfortable currents in the backwater. When you're dealing with changing water levels, today's barren water can be tomorrow's place to fish.

That boulder you're leaning against is another good example of what I'm saying. Right now, it's high and dry, but during spring runoff, the stream rises to meet the watermark, and it would spawn a rotating eddy. That stagnant pool at your feet, in the early spring, is a very likely place to catch a trout.

Baitfishing conditions are as changeable as the face of a stream, and you have to change with them. That's another reason why, to be a good fisherman, you have to learn to understand rather than learning by rote.

Ever notice how fresh and clean things smell after a storm like that? The earth was hot, and the rain cooled it, and now it is radiant with the sweet mix of both. And how that low sunlight filters through the trees . . . when you move through the openings everything is as gold as melted butter. Warm colors. Evening light is soft, warm, and gentle. It smooths the jagged edges of everything.

This should be far enough. Look how the portal walls of the canyon are catching the sunlight, and how the water sparkles blue and gold, where Back Brook flushes into the valley. It almost makes you forget about fishing, an evening like this; but not quite. I'm feeling very friendly about Back Brook at the moment.

Get yourself rigged up, and I'll explain the whys of what you're doing as you go. The name of the game is upriver bait control. You cast upstream along flow lines, just like flycasting and spinfishing, then guide the speed and drift of your bait with your rod tip and your rate of line intake. But it really starts before you ever make the first cast, with the way you assemble your terminal rigging.

The basic arrangement on the end of your line is a splitshot pinched a foot above a hook. When I'm using worms, nymphs, crickets, or grubs for bait, I prefer a single baitholder hook of sufficient size to pierce the bait fully with the tip of the hook barely protruding from the body. The barbs on the shank of a baitholder hook keep the bait from sliding down to the bend and exposing a lot of bare metal, and I've found a protruding point is far more likely to find a home in a light biter than a point buried inside a lot of meat.

It's quite important to match the hook size to the body size of the bait. The distance between point and shank should be the same as the diameter of a worm's body, or the thorax of a cricket. On a big nightcrawler, that would mean a #6 or #4 hook, on a cricket, a #10 or #12. That's the reason why you're picking through such an assortment of hooks.

When I'm using big grasshoppers or minnows, however, I prefer a double needle hook. They have a long shank with two hooks sprouting from the bend at roughly right angles to each other. The eye of the hook is a flattened, sharp-pointed needle with a small hole drilled through it. You spear the shank through the bait, then a small clip and eye passes through the hole in the needle point. You tie your line onto the eye on the clip.

With this device the same rules apply; use a hook size as large in the bend as your bait is high, but rig the bait so that the points ride up, cradling it between the hooks. This helps hide the metal, and it discourages snagging.

In order for your bait to be its most appealing, it must be moving, and you have to put it close to the fish. Remember, when the water gets dirty, trout begin to rely on odor as much as sight to identify food. As always, they'll be on the bottom, and in the same stations that you fished to before; sleepers, two-dimensional eddies, bank eddies, broken bars . . . hydraulics rather than flat water.

The closer you can drift your bait to these waiting fish, the more likely they'll be to pick it up, so you want your bait to get down, yet you can't have so much weight that you snag up and stop the natural drift.

Eventually, you'll have enough practice at reading water, and judging its relationship to your weighting, that you'll hit the right combination of lead without any testing, but at first, you'll have to experiment. The best weights to use are those splitshots with a beak in the rear . . . the kind that open as easily as they close. Even when you get good at weighting, you'll find these are a blessing because you still might have to change your splitshot as you move into a new hydraulic.

The test for correct weighting lies in the tap of the lead along the bottom. Make the test with a baited hook, as its specific gravity, in part, affects the depth of drift. A big grasshopper, for example, requires more lead to sink it deep than a worm.

If your terminal tackle flows at the same rate of speed as the current, and you feel no bounce of the bottom, you're too light. If you bounce bottom, hang up a lot, and your bait is drifting at less than half the current's speed, you've got too much lead. If you feel a regular tap-tap as the lead brushes the tops of rocks, then drifts free, and your rig is moving at around three-quarters of the speed of the current, you've hit the combination of lead and bait right on the button.

Realize too, that it is quite conceivable that the "right"

weighting might well be no weight at all ... or even a small bubble float. We've seen half a dozen places here on Back Brook that are so slow-moving that the weight of a worm and hook alone is enough for a bottom-brushing drift. In this same water, heavy baits like crawfish, or big minnows like sculpin, would have to be held up off the bottom with a water-filled plastic float weighted to neutral buoyancy.

Eight-pound test is my choice for line weight, and is a kind of compromise. There are some benefits to be derived from lighter lines; you're lobbing some pretty light baits around, and you need all the reach you can get to work distant stations. The lighter the line you use, the longer the cast. There's also the matter of line resistance in the water. The thicker the diameter of the line you use, the greater the purchase of the current. If it becomes too great, it begins to lead your bait. You lose control, and a natural deep drift. But 8-pound test turns in at least a satisfactory performance, and I can keep it under control in all but the fastest currents. The advantage it affords is strength. Even when a cast is perfectly executed and the water read with clockwork precision, there will be times when you snag up. Eight-pound test has proven to be the lightest line weight capable of wrenching hooks or splitshot loose of arresting entanglements before breaking. Breakage does happen, but not nearly so regularly as with lighter lines.

There are also two special casts you'll have to learn to make the most of this form of baitfishing, the "bait" or "soft" cast, and the pendulum cast. Go ahead and bait up, and I'll explain how they work. No reason why you shouldn't fish and learn at the same time.

The soft cast is a very different matter from the snap or fast cast. You bring the rod tip up and back very slowly until it hits about a Three O'clock position. The bait should be 18 to 24 inches from your rod tip. Propel the bait by way of a forward cast only, and through a smooth acceleration of the rod shaft.

This is why a parabolic shaft is so important. When you make this kind of cast, you'll get maximum velocity from a shaft that's working all the way down to the reel seat. The smoothness of this cast, and its gradual acceleration, help hold together soft baits.

After the line is released, coordinate your target and the sailing bait in the same way you did with a lure.

The pendulum or underhand cast is useful for working stations that are close at hand. One big advantage to baitfishing is that fish can't see you because of the cloudy water; consequently, it makes good sense to cover attractive stations that are only six feet away. As a matter of fact, I've taken a surprising number of trophy-class trout at just those kinds of distances. It suggests that there is something about being able to see well that these wise old giants depend on to outwit fishermen. That's another reason I'm so strong on the ability to lay a lot of line out when I'm fly- or lure fishing.

To make the pendulum cast, open your bail, and mend the line just as if you were handling a fly rod. The bait should be around three feet from your rod tip, and you should be holding in the neighborhood of four feet of mended line; two feet from your butt guide to your hand, two feet from your hand to the reel.

Now swing the bait like a pendulum, toward you and out, toward you and out. When it feels right, when the bait is poised in the air, ready to change direction and swing out, flip the rod tip up and release the line. You'll get maximum distance on a pendulum cast by accelerating the bait through a tug on the line with your mending hand at this instant, just like hauling a fly line.

Depending on the power you impart to the cast, and the arc of the pendulum swing, you'll be able to drop a bait anywhere between six and 35 feet. Beyond that distance, you graduate to soft cast ranges.

You look all cocked and ready to go. Have you locked in on a target? Then read the water carefully first. Do you see how the river comes into this bend swift and smooth, then suddenly slows and gets choppy 30 feet offshore? That looks like a broken bar. Cast 10 feet beyond the chop. I'll tell you what to do next.

Well placed! Slap the bail closed and take in slack. Keep reeling so that no slack develops as the bait drifts down toward you, but not so fast that you're leading the bait.

It will help if you hold your rod tip high, with both your hands above your head. This raises most of your line out of the water. You can identify a bite more quickly, and the purchase of the current on your line, and its effect, are held to a minimum.

Achieving a free drift does create one problem in that it dictates neutral resistance between your reel and the end of your line. When you're lure fishing, you always reel faster than the current, so there is some degree of pressure exerted by the line against the reel spool. It goes on in tight, even laps. Drift fishing often loops loose coils on your spool, and if you don't correct for them, you'll find you get a lot of bird's nests.

They'll be especially evident if you have too much line on the spool. It shouldn't be built up higher than ¼-inch from the forward lip. It will also help if you remember to pinch the line between your thumb and index finger as you take in the slack line at the start of a drift. Glance down at the spool before making each cast. Any loose loops of line should be easy to see. If they have formed, you can remove them by casting cross-current, then reeling in the current-tightened line.

Do you see how slack is developing at a slower rate than right after the bait plopped down? Your bait has sunk close to bottom, and it's moving along through slower planes of flow. Can you feel the occasional tick of bottom? Then keep your eye on the point where your line enters the water.

At first, you might have difficulty discerning the bounce of bottom from a nibbling fish. Bottom bounce will generally be a gentle rapping telegraphed through your rod tip. It can also be described as a rap and smooth tug; the lead hits a rock, then goes up and over the top. A fish, on the other hand, brings the bait to a smooth stop as he takes it in his mouth, then raps hard on your line as he shakes his head and chews. Another giveaway; if your line isn't moving toward you, yet you still feel the bounce of the bottom, there's got to be something down there tugging at your bait.

This is the beauty of that high visibility Stren . . . it's easy to follow under all conditions of light. So long as the line is moving, the tic-tic-tic you feel will be the shot tapping bottom, but if it stops and you still feel the ticking, that's a fish.

I see by your rod tip that the ticking has stopped entirely. If you feel pressure building against your line, and your rod bends deep but there is no bounce, you've picked up a snag. Drop your rod tip for an instant, then bring it up sharply. This will break you loose most of the time, although you'll often lose your bait. If there's no change in pressure and no ticking sensation, but your line is still drifting, your bait is up off the bottom.

It also helps to track the point where the line enters the water with your rod tip. That will keep some slack out too. When you no longer feel the tap of bottom, it's time to start another drift. The appeal of a high-drifting bait is almost nil.

Your last drift looked perfect. Did you feel the bottom? And the moment when the bait came up? Then you have the technique down. Go ahead and cast again to the same spot. If the fish are on feed, you should get a bite on one of these drifts.

When you're free-drift baitfishing on a river, you don't cover nearly the water that you do when you're using artificials. Look for ideal conditions, and work them hard. Broken bars, rotating eddies, bank eddies, and the heads of runs make for the best prospecting, but any station in a stream holds the potential for a trout.

As a rule, however, the smaller the hole or hydraulic, the less time you should spend on it, and I tend to work things like pillow-sized sleepers, two-dimensional eddies, and bucket-sized rotating eddies with one pendulum cast. The amount of fish-holding water around these formations doesn't justify a long cast and long drift. Pendulum casts are also well suited to small streams; any place where conditions suggest you're better off banging away.

Uh-uuh. That cast wasn't quite right, and it appears that you noticed it. You dropped your bait too far outside the flow line, and the angle between you and your bait kept it up off the bottom. Didn't feel a single tic, did you? Try your next cast a little closer to shore.

Another piece of advice I hope you'll take is to keep a fresh bait. When a worm loses life or a grasshopper gets bedraggled, they won't get the strikes a new bait will. This is more support for the appeal of odor. When you fish one bait for a long period of time, you eventually launder it clean.

I once took an artificial fly and squished it around with real nymphs. Messy business. But it caught fish in roily water; one on the second cast and another five minutes later. Then nothing for half an hour, so I squished some more. Bang! Another fish.

Elated with this discovery, I then tried the technique in a smaller, swollen stream. I screened the water, matched the nymphs floating down as closely as I could with an artificial, and dredged it in a crushed worm. Damned if it didn't catch fish . . . at least more than I would normally have expected on a fly. Subsequent puttering around also proved positive, with the flavor of a beefsteak and an onion, of all things. Amusing exercises, but beyond that there isn't a hell of a lot to be gained by dunking artificials in goo. Roily water is tailor-made for bait, and when you try to bend this relationship in other directions, it's going to cost you trout.

Hold it . . . You've got a bite! See how your line has stopped moving, but the tip of your rod is bouncing? Can you feel it? Then quickly, drop your rod tip. That second's worth of slack gives the trout a chance to get the bait fully in his mouth. If you don't do that, the bait keeps drifting, and they'll bite short half the time. Now wait until the current draws the line up tight and as soon as you feel the fish tug again, set the hook.

There! A hard tug. . . . strike now!

Fish on! A rainbow and a magnificent jump! Did you see that red slab of a side catch the sunlight? There is no trout that can match the sheer guts of a rainbow on the end of a line!

Keep that tip up, or you'll be fighting the river and the fish at the same time, and if he jumps again, remember to bow to him. Give him as much slack as you can while he's in the air; reach out to him with your rod tip and bend at the waist. That way a jumping fish is less likely to throw a hook.

There he goes again . . . bow!

Stu Apte taught me that trick with tarpon, and I carried it over to trout. I don't really know how necessary it is with smaller fish, but I like to do it anyway, almost as a gesture of respect. A fine fish deserves no less.

A third time! That's a strong fish. Every time I see a trout do that my heart jumps into my mouth, and a kind of mental camera clicks to freeze him at the apogee of his leap. It's like looking into a bright lightbulb and then a dark room; the image of the fish, curled, curved, and surrounded by a corona of exploding spray, stays fixed on your retina for a while. The image fades with time, but it is never quite gone. You never forget a rainbow like that, vaulting in the sun.

He's finally tiring, swinging downcurrent and into the bank. He might jump once more when he sees the net, but it won't be high or mighty. Don't beach him. If there's a chance you want to let the fish go, use your net. If he's hooked in a vital area, beaching the fish can kill him. His dead weight, resisting the tug of the line, and the consequence of flips and flops, can tear gills or flesh. Just let him loll in the current, and when he turns side-up, slip the net under him and up. There! He's yours.

A beautiful rainbow. Around 16-inches, and a pound-and-a-half. And hooked in the jaw! When you come to understand baitfishing well, you'll be able to hook trout in the jaw 80 percent of the time. The trick is strictly one of timing . . . to know how long it takes from the first hesitant tug of a trout at your bait for the fish to have it fully in his mouth. If you strike at that instant, you'll jaw-hook them every time. If you wait too long, they'll swallow the bait.

You appear to be debating whether to kill the fish or not. Don't debate too long. But if you were to ask me, I'd let the fish go. Of course, I have caught many more trout than you, and I can afford to be generous. When I first learned how to fish, I kept *everything*. The bloodlust of youth. Every good fisherman and every good hunter I know today went through it. But I have another reason. I think we've finally cracked the code, and if indeed it is bait that the trout want, I know a place nearby where we can catch a dozen beautiful brookies in as many minutes. If you want to eat trout, they're finest in a frying pan, without question.

You agree? Good. Now I just hope I can deliver on my boast. I once took my father troutfishing, and he caught a beautiful rainbow like yours on the first cast . . . one of the biggest he ever caught. "Let him go, Dad," I said. "If they're biting like that, we'll limit out in an hour."

We fished the whole day, and never had another bite. Dad still tells the story with a twinkle in his eye to everyone I introduce him to, especially if I'm going to guide them.

Go ahead, bait up and cast to that spot again. This moment has been a long time coming. The trout are on feed, we know what they want, and you have surely earned this moment on the stream. Isn't this the real glory? To earn the fish?

Another bite. I knew it! Even I'm feeling it now. Do you understand what I said about being plugged into the stream? The feeling's there now, isn't it? You know you can't miss. You've cracked the code, and you're in perfect harmony with the sights and smells and rhythms and currents that have been eluding us all day. There is nothing more to do but catch them. They're yours for the taking.

Ah! You know that feeling too? I'm extremely pleased that you do. Odd people, sportsmen. We've worked hard for this moment all day long, and now that it's here, we don't take advantage of it. It's because we measure ourselves more by what we don't take than by what we do, and because victory is assured, so the sport is really over.

You could stay here and catch your limit, we both know that. But it's anticlimactic, and it's been a long day. Besides, if it's supper you want, I know an even better place.

We'd better go there directly, then. It isn't far from here, but it's getting late. You can always come back to this; you now know the principles, and those are what ultimately catch trout. And I have one thing left to show you; it's easiest to see in this next spot. Just follow me.

/ *Epilogue*

We barely noticed this tributary on the way in, remember? The tiny trickle that spun up the valley when we turned into the canyon. Tiny streams are overlooked by practically everybody, and they're as lovely as anything we've seen today.

This thick brush puts people off, too. Which reminds me, don't wait for me to hold it out of the way for you. I'm not being unkind, just careful. You start getting used to me doing that, and you don't watch what's coming. I get my signals crossed, or forget to hang on ... it can happen ... and whap! You catch a branch across your face. With these prickly hawthorns, that wouldn't be funny. So stay well behind me, out of the range of recovering limbs. We don't have much farther to go; just another hundred yards up this little valley and the country will open up.

I don't know how often I've done this kind of thing ... just followed some nameless stream for a while to see what was over the next hill ... but it's a habit that has had rewards greater than

my efforts. There have been washouts, sure, but there have also been triumphs as sweet as a honeysuckle; little trickles of discovery that were indescribably rich.

Just a little farther now. See how the tunnel of brush lightens ahead? That's where the fishing begins.

Small streams can be very deceptive things. You'd think they'd only turn up tiny trout, but big fish are in a lot of them. Rainbows and cutthroat spawn here in the spring, and Dolly Varden come up in the summer. In the fall, browns and brookies mate in this water, and there are other things that will send big trout scooting here from down below; high water, summer heat . . .

I wouldn't bank on anything big today, though. Just some pan-sized trout. I've saved them for last because, in a way, they're the most enjoyable of all, and they're the best eating when they're so fresh that they curl as they fry.

There's no special trick to fishing most small streams. The same things we did below work on them, though it's more fun if you scale down your tackle. But this little rivulet dictates a slightly different approach. It runs like a crooked crack in the meadow, with steep grassy banks. You can't do any casting, and reading water is a superfluous exercise. When you can step across a stream with a normal stride, you've got to get right down with the fish.

I would really prefer to have a fly rod, but the bait rod will do. The main thing is that it should be long, so you can get back from the bank. Go ahead and bait up with another nightcrawler, but don't use the whole thing. Clip a piece of the worm off, long enough to thread over the shank of the hook, leaving about an inch of tail. If you use a longer chunk of worm, it will take these little trout half the evening to chew their way up to the hook.

The hook you used before is fine . . . the best, in fact. Trickle trout aren't the most sophisticated fish in the world, and they don't seem to mind the metal a bit. A #4 baitholder makes it highly unlikely that you'll hook the real small fry . . . 3 and 4 inch stuff.

The sinker is fine, too; it makes it easier to direct your bait just where you want it to go . . . most of the time you'll be fishing right off your rod tip.

We must approach the bank very quietly. Camouflage is the name of this game. You'll be right on top of the fish, and you've got to remain hidden. Bank vibrations are another thing to be careful of. Walk very quietly, rolling your weight onto the balls of your feet. These marshy meadow streams wind through topsoil that is often the consistency of jelly, and while these trout aren't wily, no trout is outright dumb.

See that sharp meander? Sneak over there and fish that worm along the outside bank. It's sure to be undercut, and if I were a fish, I'd pick that spot to bring me a lot of food. Careful now, keep a low profile, and remember where your shadow is falling. The sun is sinking fast, and you're casting a long one.

Stay as far back from the bank as you can. Let your rod do the reaching for you. Now open your bail, and drop your line straight down. When the shot hits bottom, lift the weight up about 6 inches, and let the worm wash in the current. Move it along slowly, right along the fence of that bank eddy. No need to move, let your rod do the leading.

Just follow the eddy along, and if nothing takes it the first time, come back and try it again. Someone will be along directly; of that I'm sure.

There he is! Your tip is bouncing harder than with that rainbow down on Back Brook. That's a great thing about brook trout . . . it seems the smaller they are, the harder they hit. Set that hook! There! Look at him bend that rod. Don't worry about landing techniques now, break him free of that water and get him up on the bank. You're fishing for your stomach, not for sport.

Pin him down . . . pin him down. That's the hardest part of this small stream fishing, getting a hammerlock on a twisting eel of a trout in knee-deep grass. Here; use this stick I picked up on the way. Crack him, creel him, and get back in the water. There's another one where he came from.

These little streams are more fun! Reminds me of being a kid

... I caught my first trout from a brook just like this one on a hook, worm and an old steel fly rod my uncle gave me. And another thing he showed me. Did you know that you can walk back from the bank with a long rod . . . a cane pole is best . . . just dipping a dry-fly in the water, and trout will tear it up? You'll never break any records in a place like this, but you'll never want for action.

Another one! Beautiful. I'll tell you how to cook those little ones. They're really the finest eating of all if you just gill and gut them, roll them in cracker crumbs, and fry them in hot fat until the tail is as crisp as a potato chip. Let them drain and cool until you can put them in your mouth, add a little salt and pepper, and you can eat them bones, head, and all. It's the truth. Nobody believes it until they try it, then once they do, you see them throw back everything over 8 inches!

Here . . . give me the rod for a minute. There's a little rotating eddy off the opposite bank that has been smiling and winking at me. A little flip of a pendulum cast will put me right in the middle of it.

You should see this! The worm barely hit the water, and a trout jumped on it. I actually saw him grab it and run. Just a little bit longer until he works down to the hook, a quick yank, and there he is. I've got him! This is really fishing!

But then it all has been . . . A very good day.

No, you keep the fish. One more will make just enough for a meal, and I can always catch a mess of them from Quicksilver Creek. I would rather you had them. It's the finest way to end a day like this, with a plateful of pan-sized trout, and the memories.

But let me ask you something for a change before we leave. Come over here, next to me. It's getting very close to dusk, but I think there's enough light to see. Let me clip a few feet off the end of this line . . . hand me a piece of worm.

Now elbow up through the grass, and part it just enough to drop this line down. Take hold of the line gently, and watch. See the ripples it makes?

Look, there he is, sleek, and bullet shaped, and perfect, easing out from under the cutbank and to the middle of the circle. See him open his mouth and take in the worm? Gently at first; now his gills and jaws work, his head snaps to the side, and he begins to tug.

The line is drawn between you once again. We talk about purism, but if there is purity in the way you catch a trout, this must be the purest moment of all. Can you feel him tugging? Do you know the real question that trout is asking?

Tell me: who is catching whom, and on which end of the line? No, I don't have that answer. All I know is that to catch a trout is to be connected to an essential ingredient of living; grasping the meaning of what is around you, and appreciating it. You and that fish are a celebration and affirmation of your own existence, and when you try to go beyond that, all distinctions fade.

I've brought you as far as I can, and I must go now, but before I leave there are still some things I want you to know. The lake we fished was Milkshake Lake, and at the head of this little stream you'll find the Goldfish Bowl. A mile below the bridge, the Gunflint joins Back Brook from the south, and Quicksilver Creek runs in from the north a half-mile further down. They are known as the Roaring River, from there to where it meets the Diamond to form the Marble three miles above the tackleshop on Highway 191. Just look for them, and you'll find them all.

No, I'm not compromising my philosophies. I count you as a friend after today, and I'll always share my knowledge with a friend, even my best trout water. Besides, I said this morning that I wouldn't give you a fish, and I don't have to anymore. You've learned to catch them on your own hook.

It's getting dark. It was just about this time of evening that we met last spring, wasn't it? Another kind of circle that we can add to the day. Go ahead, you lead the way for a change. You know the path as well as I do by now.

Index